Reserve Retirement Reform

A Viewpoint on Recent Congressional Proposals

Beth J. Asch, James Hosek, David S. Loughran

Prepared for the Office of the Secretary of Defense

NATIONAL DEFENSE RESEARCH INSTITUTE

The research described in this report was prepared for the Office of the Secretary of Defense (OSD). The research was conducted in the RAND National Defense Research Institute, a federally funded research and development center sponsored by the Office of the Secretary of Defense, the Joint Staff, the Unified Combatant Commands, the Department of the Navy, the Marine Corps, the defense agencies, and the defense Intelligence Community under Contract DASW01-01-C-0004.

Library of Congress Cataloging-in-Publication Data

Asch, Beth J.
    Reserve retirement reform : a viewpoint on recent congressional proposals / Beth Asch, James Hosek,
David Loughran.
      p. cm.
    Includes bibliographical references.
    "TR-199."
    ISBN 0-8330-3693-9 (pbk. : alk. paper)
    1. United States—Armed Forces—Reserves. 2. United States—Armed Forces—Appointments and retirements.
I. Hosek, James R. II. Loughran, David S., 1969– III.Title.

UA42.A7323 2004
331.25'2135537'0973—dc22

2004024941

The RAND Corporation is a nonprofit research organization providing objective analysis and effective solutions that address the challenges facing the public and private sectors around the world. RAND's publications do not necessarily reflect the opinions of its research clients and sponsors.

RAND® is a registered trademark.

Published 2006 by the RAND Corporation
1776 Main Street, P.O. Box 2138, Santa Monica, CA 90407-2138
1200 South Hayes Street, Arlington, VA 22202-5050
4570 Fifth Avenue, Suite 600, Pittsburgh, PA 15213
RAND URL: http://www.rand.org/
To order RAND documents or to obtain additional information, contact
Distribution Services: Telephone: (310) 451-7002;
Fax: (310) 451-6915; Email: order@rand.org

PREFACE

The nation's growing reliance on the Reserves has kindled interest in the adequacy of reserve compensation, and this interest has grown as a consequence of the recent, heavy deployments of reservists to Afghanistan and Iraq. At the same time, there has been a long-standing concern in the reserve community about the lack of equity between reserve retirement benefits and active-duty retirement benefits. In 2003 Congress introduced four bills that, although differing in detail, all had the objective of increasing the generosity of reserve retirement benefits. Among the motives behind this proposed legislation were to diminish the apparent inequity between reserve and active-duty retirement benefits and to increase the compensation of reservists in light of the increased role they are now called on to play in the nation's defense.

Within this landscape, this paper discusses the issue of equity in reserve versus active-duty retirement benefits and attempts to broaden the terms of policy discussion. We consider the increase in reserve deployments that has occurred over the 1990s and spiked in the period since September 11, 2001, and we identify and discuss other issues that we believe should be considered in concert with the proposed changes in reserve retirement benefits. These issues include the role of compensation in shaping the reserve personnel force structure, the importance of mechanisms permitting the Reserves to manage its personnel more flexibly than it does today, the urgency of ensuring the supply of reservists—the addition of new personnel and the retention of experienced personnel—in view of their currently more extensive and longer deployments, and the relationship of reserve retirement reforms to the many past proposals to reform active-duty retirement benefits. We also offer views on the likely retention effects and cost of the congressional proposals. Finally, we review proposals to reform the active-duty military retirement system recommended by past commissions and study groups to better understand how these proposals relate to the current reserve retirement system.

The research presented in this paper is part of a larger project intended to develop and apply a modeling capability to assess the effect of changes in reserve retirement benefits, and potentially other aspects of reserve and active-duty compensation, on active-duty retention, the flow from actives to Reserves, reserve retention of prior and nonprior service personnel (allowing for movement in and out of reserve components), and cost.

The information and discussion contained in this paper should be of interest to the defense manpower policy and research communities, including members of Congress active in national security affairs and their staff members; the leadership and personnel experts in the armed forces; external organizations and researchers interested in defense manpower, compensation, and the role and reform of retirement benefit structures; and members of the media who cover the armed forces and the issues of retirement reform and the impact of deployments on retention.

This research was conducted for the deputy assistant secretary of defense for reserve affairs (manpower and personnel) and for the Office of Compensation, Office of the Under Secretary of Defense for Personnel and Readiness within the Forces and Policy Resources Center of the RAND Corporation's National Defense Research Institute, a federally funded research and development center sponsored by the Office of the Secretary of Defense, the Joint Staff, the unified commands, and the defense agencies.

Comments are welcome and may be addressed to the project leaders, Beth Asch at Beth_Asch@rand.org, or James Hosek at James_Hosek@rand.org, or by mail at RAND Corporation, 1776 Main Street, Santa Monica, CA 90407-2138.

For more information on RAND's Forces and Policy Resources Center, contact the director, James Hosek. He can be reached by email above; by phone, at 310-393-0411, extension 7183; or by mail at RAND, 1776 Main Street, Santa Monica, CA 90407-2138. More information about RAND is available at www.rand.org.

CONTENTS

FIGURES AND TABLES

Figures

Tables

SUMMARY

A consequence of the more intensive use of the reserve components in national defense in recent years has been greater attention paid to the adequacy and efficiency of the reserve compensation system. A key component of this system is the reserve retirement plan that pays, beginning at age 60, an annuity to qualified reservists who have completed 20 years of creditable service (YCS). Four bills were introduced in Congress in 2003 to reduce the age when reservists can begin to receive retirement benefits. One proposal would allow reservists to begin receiving retirement pay immediately upon completing 20 YCS, with the last six years as a member of a reserve component. Two related proposals would lower the retirement annuity age to 55. Another would set the retirement age on a sliding scale that depended on years of service (YOS); those with more YOS can retire earlier, as early as age 53.

This paper draws from past research as well as from our ongoing project on military retirement to provide input regarding these proposals and the broader issues surrounding reserve retirement reform. We argue that the issues surrounding the reform of the active and reserve retirement systems must go beyond the single consideration of the age of benefit entitlement. To that effect, we discuss the relative merit of reserve retirement alternatives in light of a range of enduring objectives related to reserve personnel management, such as equity, cost-effectiveness, and improved force management. We find that the case for proposed reforms based on equity is ambiguous; given the differences in the demands of active and reserve service, one would not expect an equitable reserve retirement system to treat reservists and active-duty members identically. Furthermore, increasing reserve retirement benefits is neither the only nor necessarily the most equitable way to compensate reservists for the risk of added deployments. Our assessment of the cost-effectiveness of proposed reforms argues in favor of providing compensation on a current rather than deferred basis. At the same time, there are potential benefits to deferring some portion of compensation (e.g., to encourage the recruitment and retention of individuals who intend to stay with the Reserves). In addition, our review of the work of past commissions and study groups devoted to the study of military retirement suggests that a wider range of proposed reforms should also be considered. In particular, to support the total force concept, reserve retirement reform will need to be integrated with active reform, although the resulting systems need not be the same for each component.

The remainder of this summary expands these arguments by discussing the rationale behind reserve retirement reform in light of five broad objectives of the reserve compensation and personnel management system. These objectives are then used to assess potential reforms.

Objective: Increase the equity of reserve retirement benefits relative to active-duty benefits

Rationale: One reason for reducing the reserve retirement annuity age is the argument that, although reservists are a fundamental part of the total force, they receive much less in retirement benefits than do active duty since the amount of reservist benefits is determined based on pro rata YOS and the payout does not begin until age 60. Given the increasingly important role of reservists in the total force and the fact that retirement benefits are based on actual service, it is unfair, the argument goes, to begin reserve retirement benefits at age 60 when active benefits begin immediately upon retirement from active duty.

Assessment: The concept of equity has many facets beyond placing years of military service on a pro rata basis or reducing the age of benefit entitlement. Among these are the demands of full-time active duty in terms of readiness, deployment, frequent absences, permanent change of station (PCS) moves, the inability to have a full-time civilian job, and the impact of the military regimen on the family and the employment and earning opportunities of the military spouse.

In addition, the calculation of basic pay in determining retirement benefits favors reservists. Basic pay for a retired reservist is the value of basic pay in effect when the reservist turns 60, not the value of basic pay in effect in the year when the reservist separated plus the cost-of-living adjustment to age 60. This favors the reservists because basic pay typically rises faster than the cost of living. Furthermore, one purpose of active-duty retirement benefits is to help the retired active-duty member establish a civilian career, whereas reservists typically already have a civilian career and a retirement benefit plan with their employer.

Finally, the choice of age 55 as well as the formulas for computing the sliding scale in the various congressional proposals are ad hoc and would do comparatively little to enhance nominal equity because there are no comparable age requirements in the active retirement system. Furthermore, these proposed changes are also ad hoc when judged from the benchmark of the two civil service retirement systems, the Civil Service Retirement System (CSRS) and the Federal Employees Retirement System (FERS), because CSRS is being phased out and the annuity age for FERS is rising to age 57.

Objective: Increase compensation because of more frequent, longer reserve deployments

   Rationale: Reserve deployments increased during the 1990s and have risen even more because of operations in Iraq and Afghanistan and the war on terrorism. More generous reserve retirement benefits would help to compensate for the added burden of deployment.

   Assessment: Increasing the generosity of reserve retirement benefits is an inefficient, poorly targeted, and unfair way of compensating for the higher burden of deployment. It is inefficient because reservists most likely have a higher rate of interest than the government rate of interest. Theory suggests that an individual's rate of interest is about equal to the individual's rate of time preference (willingness to trade off consumption today for consumption tomorrow, also called *personal discount rate*), provided consumption is not changing much from year to year. Estimates of military members' rate of time preference are of 20 to 30 percent per year. This compares with a government interest rate of 3 percent or 4 percent (rates adjusted for inflation). At a 3.5 percent rate of interest, the government would need to set aside $0.71 now in order to pay $1 in ten years. But from the viewpoint of a reservist with even a 10 percent rate of time preference, the present value of that dollar to be received ten years from now is $0.39, and at a 20 percent rate it is only $0.16. Therefore, the present value of the benefit cost to the government ($0.71) is much higher than the present value of the benefit to the reservist (say $0.39).

   Using retirement benefits to address the stress of greater deployment is poorly targeted because more generous retirement benefits would potentially reward all reservists, even those with little or no deployment. A majority of reservists have not been mobilized in recent operations, including Operations Noble Eagle, Enduring Freedom, and Iraqi Freedom, in Iraq and Afghanistan. Furthermore, embedding compensation in retirement benefits is also unfair because most of the reservists who deploy are younger personnel, and most of the younger personnel do not stay in the Reserves long enough to qualify for these benefits.

Objective: Ensure adequate supply of reserve personnel

   Rationale: Reserve deployments have been far more extensive than reservists expected, and the dates of departure for and return from deployment have been uncertain. Reservists might not be willing to be away from home as often as now anticipated (9 to 12 months every 4 to 5 years rather than every 7 to 8 years). Also, employers might become wary of placing reservists in positions of significant responsibility; recognizing this, some reservists might opt to leave the Reserves rather than jeopardize their civilian career advancement.

Assessment: Increasing the generosity of reserve retirement benefits is an inefficient and poorly targeted way to improve reserve retention or recruiting. Even if reserve retirement benefits started around age 55 instead of at age 60, the present value to reservists (and potential recruits) age 20 to 40 would be small, and the effect on their recruiting and retention would be small. Older reservists near 20 YOS would reap the biggest gain from an increase in retirement benefits, but their retention rates are typically quite high, so for them too the increase in retention would be small. The fact that many junior reservists will not stay in the Reserves long enough to qualify for retirement benefits implies that an increase in retirement benefits will be of little consequence to them. In contrast, an increase in current pay would be of full and immediate value to a reservist and therefore can be expected to have a much greater effect on the retention and recruiting of junior personnel.

Objective: Increase flexibility of managing reserve personnel

Rationale: Reserve deployments have been far more extensive than reservists expected, and the dates of departure for and return from deployment have been uncertain. Some reservists might not be willing to accept a continuation of the high rates of deployment and long tours that have occurred under Operation Iraqi Freedom and Operation Enduring Freedom.[1] Also, employers might become wary of placing reservists in positions of significant responsibility; recognizing this, some reservists might opt to leave the reserves rather than jeopardize their civilian career advancement.

Assessment: The reserve compensation and personnel management systems are stable, visible, scalable, and equitable in providing similar compensation and career advancement opportunity to personnel

---

[1] The possibility of a continuation of higher deployments is inherent in the testimony of Lieutenant General Helmly, chief of the Army Reserve: "We are committed to achieving a capability ratio that will manage Army Reserve deployments to once every four or five years." This statement is also an indication of the effort within the Army Reserve to transform into a more readily deployable force. Whether the future will actually require deployments once every four or five years, versus a longer period, is an open question. (Statement by LTG James R. Helmly, Chief, Army Reserve, Department of the Army, before the Subcommittee on Personnel, Committee on Personnel, United States

given their YOS and responsibility and regardless of their military occupation. These systems have resulted in highly similar retention profiles by occupation.

As the active-duty and reserve components transform, it may be preferable to encourage longer careers in some occupations and to create greater opportunities and incentives for innovation in every occupation. Doing this may require changes in the compensation and personnel management systems. The current reserve retirement benefit system, like the active-duty retirement benefit system, encourages similarity and conformity in careers, retention, and incentives. In particular, it encourages personnel to complete 20 YCS, and it offers weaker incentives to serve more than 20 years. As long as retirement benefits depend only on pay grade and pro rata YOS, they will not be a means of inducing greater variation in reserve careers and retention. Also, because reservists discount retirement benefits, a $1 increase in retirement benefits will have less incentive effect than a $1 increase in current compensation. On net, increasing the generosity of reserve retirement benefits does not provide a direct or cost-effective way to increase the flexibility of personnel management, whereas increasing current pay through special and incentive pay and revising the personnel management system can increase that flexibility.

Objective: Ensure cost-effectiveness of reserve compensation system

Rationale: A compensation system should be cost-effective. If it is not, then the cost of personnel is higher than it needs to be.

Assessment: Because of the difference between a reservist's interest rate and the government's interest rate, the present value of $1 of deferred compensation will be far less to the reservist than the present value of the government's cost of providing it. This argues in favor of providing compensation on a current basis rather than on a deferred basis.

Using data on reserve personnel for fiscal years (FY) 1999 and 2000, we computed the per-capita present discounted costs and present discounted values of the congressional retirement proposals to reduce the annuity age for enlisted and officer retirees assuming a real government interest rate of 2.5 percent, a rate of real-wage growth of 1 percent, and a 10 percent personal interest rate. We found that the per-capita cost of the current retirement system is dramatically less than the per-capita cost under the immediate annuity and age-55 proposals

Senate, Second Session, 108th Congress, Active and Reserve Personnel Programs, March 31, 2004, p. 16.)

($144,516 versus $219,415 and $179,677). The per-capita cost of the sliding-age alternative is the least expensive of the three alternatives ($155,573), reflecting the low prevalence of new retirees below age 60 with sufficient YOS to qualify for retirement at ages below 60 on the sliding-age scale. The discounted present values of the alternatives are substantially lower than the cost figures. For example, the present value of the current system for a retiree is $45,845, much less than the $144,516 cost. Clearly, the typical retiree values retirement benefits less than what it costs to provide them, and, depending on the personal interest rate, the difference is substantial.

These results argue in favor of providing compensation on a current basis rather than on a deferred basis. On the other hand, it is important to recognize that it can be cost-effective to defer some portion of compensation. Deferred compensation can encourage the recruitment and retention of individuals who intend to stay with the Reserves; provide an incentive for complying with organizational norms of behavior and behavior standards (versus being dismissed for improper or insubordinate behavior); provide an incentive to exert effort and seek promotion (because retirement benefits are higher); and induce the most senior personnel to separate, clearing the promotion channels for junior personnel. Increasing the generosity of reserve retirement benefits would strengthen the capability to perform these roles. However, there are also alternative approaches. Current compensation and personnel management can be structured to create greater incentives for recruiting, retention, effort, and separation. Finding the right balance between current and deferred compensation therefore requires an analysis of the costs and effects of specific policy alternatives.

Finally, from the perspective of congressional action in a tight budget situation, increasing the generosity of reserve retirement benefits is a way of acting today on behalf of reservists while deferring the payment for the action until tomorrow. That is, increasing *deferred* military compensation might be politically more attractive than (further) increasing current military compensation.

Toward the Development of Retirement Reform Alternatives

Numerous study groups and commissions have discussed reforms to the military retirement system, especially the active system, to address problems of cost, equity, and management flexibility. Concerns have focused on such issues as the cost of providing retirement benefits immediately as active members transition from the military to their second career in the civilian sector; the lack of retirement benefits for members who serve but not long enough to be eligible for military retirement; the differences between the defined benefit plan provided by the military and those plans prevalent in the civilian sector; and the one-size-fits-all retirement system. These issues are also relevant to though not always in the forefront of discussion about reserve retirement reform.

Moreover, to support the total force concept, it is clear that retirement reform for both the active and reserve components must work in concert to achieve their respective personnel goals. Assessments of alternative reforms must also consider how to address obstacles to reform, such as the lack of a consensus for change.

ACKNOWLEDGMENTS

We would like to thank Scott Seggerman at the Defense Manpower Data Center and Virginia Hyland in the Office of the Assistant Secretary of Defense for Reserve Affairs, for their generous help in providing information on reserve component deployments. We thank Phoenix Do for fine research assistance. We benefited significantly from the comments and reviews from Susan Hosek and Nicole Maestas at RAND and from Paul Hogan at the Lewin Group. We appreciate the assistance we received from our project monitors, Richard Krimmer, Director of Military Personnel Programs, Office of the Assistant Secretary of Defense for Reserve Affairs, and Captain Michael Price, Assistant Director of Military Personnel (Compensation) and Coast Guard Liaison to the Office of the Assistant Secretary of Defense for Reserve Affairs. We also benefited from the input of Mr. Wayne Spruell, former Principal Director, Manpower and Peronnel, and Mr. Tom Bush, the current Principal Director for Manpower and Personnel within the Office of the Assistant Secretary of Defense for Reserve Affairs. Finally, we wish to thank Dr. John Winkler, Deputy Assistant Secretary of Defense for Reserve Affairs (Manpower and Personnel), for his sponsorship of our project and his input to this research.

LIST OF ABBREVIATIONS

AFQT	Armed Forces Qualification Test
AGR	Active Guard Reserve
CPI	consumer price index
CSRS	Civil Service Retirement System
DC	defined contribution
DEERS	Defense Enrollment Eligibility Reporting System
DMDC	Defense Manpower Data Center
DoD	Department of Defense
DRM	dynamic retention model
DSB	Defense Science Board
ESGR	Employer Support for the Guard and Reserve
FERS	Federal Employees Retirement System
FY	fiscal year
IDT	inactive-duty training
ODS	Operation Desert Storm
PCS	permanent change of station
QRMC	Quadrennial Review of Military Compensation
RCCPDS	Reserve Components Common Personnel Data System
RCS	Reserve Components Survey
TSP	thrift savings plan
USERRA	Uniformed Services Employment and Reemployment Rights Act
YCS	years of creditable service
YOS	years of service

CHAPTER ONE: INTRODUCTION

Since the 1980s, the reserve components increasingly have been called on to contribute to national defense. Measured in terms of man-days, the Reserves contribution rose from an estimated .9 million duty days in 1986 to 17.1 million in 2001. Reservists have been called to support homeland defense; contingency operations in Bosnia, Kosovo, and Southwest Asia; humanitarian assistance in Africa and Central America; disaster relief; and counter-drug operations. More recently, as a result of Operation Enduring Freedom in Afghanistan and Operations Noble Eagle, Enduring Eagle, and Iraqi Freedom in Iraq, duty days rose to 23.9 million in 2002 with almost 418,750 mobilizations as of August 2004.[2] Today the Department of Defense (DoD) relies on the reserve components to carry out virtually all elements of our national security strategy. Indeed, many military capabilities exist only in the Reserves.

As a result of the dramatic increase in usage, the typical Selected Reserve member can expect more frequent and longer call-ups than in the 1980s and 1990s. This heightened risk of deployment together with an improving civilian labor market may adversely affect the ability of the Reserves to recruit high-quality reservists, attract skilled personnel leaving active duty, and retain experienced personnel in key occupations. Retirement compensation is one tool the Reserves have for meeting these accession and retention challenges.

The reserve retirement system has remained largely unchanged since its inception in 1948. Like the active-duty retirement system, it rewards reservists who complete 20 years of service (YOS) with a retirement annuity based on pro rata YOS and basic pay. Unlike active-duty retirees, though, reserve retirees are not eligible to receive this annuity until their sixtieth birthday. Active-duty retirees receive their annuity immediately upon separation.[3] This apparent inequity between the active-duty and reserve retirement systems, long an issue for reservists, has become more prominent in recent years as the distinction between reserve and active-duty service erodes. Thus, the call for reserve retirement reform comes from reservists who feel they are treated unfairly vis-à-vis their active-duty peers and from the reserve components who question whether current reserve compensation, including retirement pay, is structured appropriately to attract and

---

[2] This figure is based on information provided by the Office of the Assistant Secretary of Defense Affairs using the Services Daily Mobilization Report. The figure includes Reserve members who are mobilized more than once.

retain reservists with desired skills and experience, and eventually to separate them from the Reserves.

In recognition of the expanded role of the reserve forces and the call for retirement reform, several bills were introduced in Congress to address reserve compensation issues and specifically the equity of reserve retirement benefits. Four bills introduced in 2003 reduce the age when qualified reservists would be entitled to begin receipt of their retirement benefits. They are

- H.R. 331—Provide an immediate annuity to eligible reservists
- H.R. 742—Lower annuity payout age from 60 to 55 with no reduction in annuity amount
- S. 1000—Revise age and eligibility requirements on a sliding scale: at 20 YOS, retire at age 60; at 22 YOS, retire at age 59; up to 34 YOS, retire at age 53; would also expand TRICARE to reservists and their families and provide tax credits for employers of reservists
- S. 1035—(Companion legislation to H.R. 742) Lower annuity payout age from 60 to 55 with no reduction in annuity amount.

This report discusses the issue of equity in reserve versus active-duty retirement benefits while attempting to broaden the terms of the policy discussion. The paper has three objectives.

First, we frame the debate about reserve retirement alternatives by highlighting a range of enduring objectives related to reserve personnel management, such as equity, cost-effectiveness, and improved force management, that must be considered when contemplating a change in the structure of military compensation. We believe the issues surrounding the reform of the active and reserve retirement systems are more complex than the single consideration of the age of benefit entitlement because the systems differ in multiple respects as do the ways and circumstances in which active and reserve members perform service.

Second, we offer a preliminary evaluation of the alternatives proposed by Congress in light of the broader objectives of reserve personnel management. Our evaluation and cost analysis indicate that none of the currently proposed reforms is likely to have more than a modest effect on reserve accessions and retention, though some could substantially increase the per-capita cost of reserve retirement. Proposals to use increased reserve retirement benefits to compensate for the greater burden of deployment borne by today's reservists are not well targeted to the vast majority of reservists who are deployed or at

---

[3] Appendix A gives an overview of the reserve and active-duty retirement systems.

risk of deployment. These reservists are typically much younger than those near retirement and in many cases will not remain in the Reserves long enough to qualify for retirement benefits.

Third, we briefly review past proposals to reform the active-duty retirement system and discuss their relevance to the reserve components. Our review suggests that many of the issues considered are relevant to the Reserves, indicating that such past proposals should be considered in the development of alternatives to reform the reserve retirement system.

The paper is organized as follows: Section 2 discusses the broad goals of reserve compensation and personnel management; Section 3 presents our initial assessment of the congressional proposals; and Section 4 presents our review of the issues addressed by past commissions and study groups.

CHAPTER TWO: OBJECTIVES OF RESERVE COMPENSATION AND RETIREMENT REFORM

Reserve retirement plays an integral role in the Reserves' personnel management system, the objective of which is to maintain a skilled and motivated reserve force capable of performing its national defense mission. Retirement benefits serve as an important incentive for the Reserves to use in meeting accession and retention objectives. Thus, in order to evaluate various proposals for reforming reserve retirement, we need to consider potential reforms in light of several broader goals of reserve personnel management. In this section, we consider reserve retirement reform in relation to five such goals:

(1) Enhancing equity

(2) Recognizing more frequent and longer deployments

(3) Ensuring adequate supply of high-quality reserve personnel with requisite skills and experience

(4) Improving management flexibility of reserve personnel

(5) Ensuring a cost-effective military compensation system

These goals are in the spirit of the principles underlying military compensation generally as developed in the sixth and seventh Quadrennial Review of Military Compensation (QRMC [see Appendix B]). They also focus on specific concerns, such as equity and longer deployments, driving the current debate about reserve retirement reform.

Equity

Few things undermine morale more in any organization than a prevailing sense that staff members are compensated unfairly. The need to convey a sense of fairness among its members is reflected in the relatively rigid schedule by which the military determines basic pay and allowances and determines promotions. As put forth in the fifth edition of the *Military Compensation Background Papers,* the principle of equity encompasses two concepts: comparability and competitiveness (U.S. DoD, 1996). Comparability implies that individuals within the uniformed services receive equal pay for equal work. Competitiveness implies that military members receive pay that is competitive with civilian opportunities. But this is not an official definition of equity, and other aspects of equity also deserve attention, such as the distinction between equality of opportunity and equality of outcome. Equality of opportunity can go hand in hand with inequality of outcome, provided that individuals are given, and believe they have, equal opportunity and that the outcomes are fair. In the military, some disparity in outcomes is commonplace, such as differences in the speed of promotion among individuals in a specialty or the payment of special or incentive pay in certain circumstances (e.g., selective reenlistment bonuses).

In recent years the issue of comparability has dominated the debate over reserve retirement. The Office of Reserve Affairs routinely receives congressional inquiries questioning why reserve members must wait until age 60 to receive retirement pay when active-duty members receive it immediately upon separation. Similarly, the four congressional bills that seek to lower the reserve retirement entitlement age reflect the same issue.

To understand the issue of equity with regard to the reserve retirement system, one must first recognize three differences between the reserve and active-duty retirement systems: age of pension receipt, calculation of pro rata YOS, and calculation of basic pay for purposes of retirement.

Age of Pension Receipt

Active-duty personnel qualify for retirement benefits when they complete 20 years of active-duty service, and they receive retirement benefits as soon as they retire from service. For example, a person entering active duty at age 20 and retiring after 22 YOS will receive retirement benefits at age 42.

Reserve personnel qualify for retirement benefits after completing 20 years of creditable service (YCS) but may not receive retirement benefits until age 60. Creditable service includes each year of active service, if any, and each creditable year of reserve service, defined as a year in which the individual earned at least 50 points. A reservist receives 15 points for being affiliated with the Ready Reserve and a point for each training drill (typically four drills one weekend each month), each day of active training (typically 14 days each summer), each day of duty when activated, and each day of various other activities such as participation in a funeral color guard. Most selected reservists have no trouble accumulating 50 points in a year, and in effect each year of participation in the Selected Reserve counts as a year of creditable service. By comparison, a person entering active duty at age 20, separating after 8 years, immediately joining the Selected Reserve, and serving 14 years continuously will have 22 YCS at age 42. But this reservist will not receive retirement benefits until age 60.

The rules for determining age of pension receipt seem to favor active-duty personnel. Because many active-duty members retire in their mid-forties, they can receive retirement benefits for about 15 years more than retired reservists. Earlier receipt increases the present discounted value of lifetime retirement pay for active-duty members relative to that of reservists because active members receive retirement pay over more years and receive it earlier in their lives.

Pro Rata Years of Service

The amount of reserve retirement benefits is based on pro rata YOS. Pro rata YOS equals the number of active years, if any, plus the total number of points accumulated in the Reserves divided by 360. For example, someone who serves 10 years in the actives and 10 years in the Reserves, earning a total of 720 points (an average of 72 points per year), has a total of 12 pro rata YOS (10 + 720/360). The reservist's retirement benefits would then be based on 12 YOS, whereas an active's retirement benefits would be based on 20 years. This difference, taken together with the later age of pension receipt for reservists, has added to perceptions of unfairness concerning reserve retirement. According to this position, pro rata YOS already adjusts for the fact that reservists are not on duty year-round, and with that taken into consideration, the argument goes, why shouldn't reservists be able to receive retirement benefits immediately upon separating from the Reserves with at least 20 creditable years?

On the other hand, the difference in how reservists earn YCS could be seen as unfair to active members. Nondeploying reservists typically earn about 70 retirement points per year, and 15 of those points, or about one-fifth, are earned for just being affiliated with the Reserves. Reservists also receive double points for each day of drilling. For active members, a day is a day in terms of points and there are no points for affiliation with an active component.

Basic Pay

The calculation of basic pay for retirement purposes also differs for reservists and active-duty members. Basic pay for the purposes of active-duty retirement is equal to the average of the member's highest 36 months, or "high-three" years, of basic pay prior to retirement. Thus, if an active-duty member retires in January 2004, basic pay for the purposes of retirement will equal his or her average pay between January 2001 and December 2003.[4] Basic pay for reservists who enter the Retired Reserve upon separating from the Ready Reserve is calculated based on the basic pay in effect for the 36 months preceding age 60.

The calculation of basic pay is to the reservist's advantage for two reasons. First, between the time of a reservist's separation from the Reserves and age 60, basic pay might increase faster than the rate of inflation. Since 1982 the average annual rate of growth in basic pay at the modal enlisted rank of retirement (E-7) has exceeded the average annual rate of growth in the consumer price index (CPI) by about 1 percent. Much of this relative real-wage growth, however, has occurred in the past few years, especially because of the large increase in basic pay in FY2000, the restructuring of the pay table in that year, and large increases since 2000. For the modal officer at retirement (O-6) annual pay growth has been about equal to the CPI. Second, reservists in the Retired Reserve continue to accumulate longevity for the purposes of calculating basic pay. So, for example, a reservist separating from the Ready Reserve at age 51 as an E-7 with 24 creditable YOS will receive retirement pay based on the basic pay in effect for an E-7 with 26 or more calendar YOS providing he or she remains in the Retired Reserve. Together, these differences can translate into noticeable differences in basic pay. For the E-7 just mentioned, FY2004 basic pay is $3,599 for 24 YOS and $3,855 for 26 or more YOS, a difference of more than $250 a month, or $3,000 a year. The CPI-adjusted value of this difference would grow larger in future years to the extent that increases in basic pay outpace increases in the cost of living.

Overall Comparison

To illustrate how these differences in retirement systems affect retirement pay, we compared the value of the reservist retirement benefits under the current retirement system and two alternatives.

---

[4] This assumes the individual does not have other months in which his or her basic pay exceeded the last 36 months of basic pay.

Figure 2.1 graphs the present discounted value of retirement pay for reservists under (1) the current reserve retirement system; (2) the active-duty retirement system with high-three averaging; and (3) the active-duty REDUX system, which we call REDUX+$30k.[5] In all three scenarios, we assume the reservist accumulates points and that YCS for the purposes of computing retired pay are based on pro rata YOS as is the policy under the current reserve retirement system.[6] In the case of REDUX+$30k, we prorate accordingly the $30,000 bonus obtained at 15 YOS. The figure uses data from the Reserve Components Common Personnel Data System (RCCPDS) on all reservists with more than 20 YOS as of September 1999, including both prior and nonprior service reservists, and the January 2004 pay table.[7] For each calendar year of service, we compute the modal enlisted and officer pay grade, median years of creditable service, median point accumulation, median time in grade, median age at separation, and average life expectancy. By using the median point accumulation we are associating a certain level of pro rata YOS with each creditable year of service. Assuming a personal interest rate of 10 percent, a real annual growth in basic pay of 1 percent, and that all retirees reach age 60 with maximum longevity, we, with these inputs, can compute the present discounted value of retirement pay under the three scenarios.[8]

---

[5] Appendix A provides an overview of the active-duty and reserve retirement systems. Briefly, active members who entered the military after July 31, 1986, can choose between a retirement system that pays an annuity after 20 years of service equal to 50 percent of their highest three years of basic pay (alternative 2) or a system (alternative 3) that pays 40 percent of their high-three pay plus a $30,000 lump-sum career-retention bonus paid at year of service 15. Alternatives 2 and 3 also have different cost-of-living adjustment provisions.

[6] For active members, retirement pay is based on creditable years of service, not pro rata years of service. By assuming that the retirement pay formula is based on pro rata years of service even for the two active systems in Figure 2.1, differences between the active and reserve systems for reservists shown in the figure are not attributable differences in the way years of service is determined in the active versus the reserve components.

[7] See Appendix C for a description of the data used.

[8] We make the simplifying assumption that all retirees have served at least 36 months at their current basic pay. This leads us to slightly overestimate the value of active-duty retirement since individuals do not necessarily separate with 36 months at their highest level of basic pay.

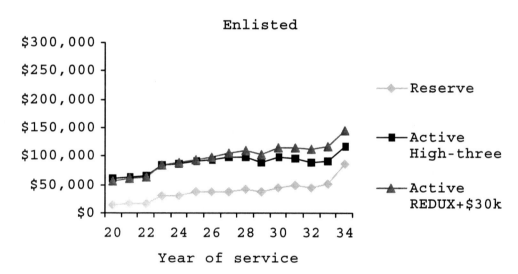

Figure 2.1—Present Discounted Value of Retired Pay

As shown, the present discounted value of retirement pay for enlisted members and officers under the current reserve retirement system at a given year of service is substantially lower than under either high-three averaging or REDUX+$30k. In fact, at any of the YOS shown, the present discounted value of retirement pay under the reserve retirement system is less than half of that under either of the active-duty systems, high-three averaging system or REDUX+$30k.

Two reasons help explain why: Reservists typically have far less than 20 pro rata YOS when they retire, but actives have at least 20 years; reserve retirement benefits do not begin until age 60, but active retirement benefits begin immediately upon retirement. We did note that the determination of basic pay favors the reservists, but the other two reasons overwhelm this factor. Consider, for example, an O-5 reservist who separates from the Reserves at age 50 with 25 creditable YOS, basic pay of $6,761 in the 2004 basic pay table, 3,146 accumulated points, and who can expect to live to age 78 (see figures in Table C.2).

- If reserve retirement benefits were based on YOS, the reservist's retirement benefits would be Y = 25 x .025 x $6,761 = $4,225 per month. But because reserve retirement benefits are based on pro rata YOS, this reservist has 3,146/360 = 8.74 years, and therefore retirement benefits are Y = 8.74 x .025 x $6,761 = $1,477 per month.

- If the reservist received benefits immediately upon separating, then, as just shown, the reservist would receive $1,477 per month. But because this 50-year-old reservist must wait 10 years to begin receiving benefits, the present value of $1,477 at a 10 percent interest rate is $576. Furthermore, the fact that no benefits are received until age 60 means that the reservist has 10 less years of benefit payments than if benefits were started immediately.

On net, these considerations lead to a far smaller present value of retirement benefits under the reserve system than under high-three or REDUX+$30k. As Figure 2.1 shows, the present value of benefits is $67k under the current reserve system, $185k under REDUX+$30k, and $192k under high-three. A similar example can be given for an enlisted person, although the difference in present values is much smaller.

Although the present value of retirement benefits is smaller than it would be under the other systems, is this result necessarily unfair? On the criterion of comparability, or equal pay for equal work, the answer depends on whether one believes reservists and active-duty members truly perform equal work. Although today reservists are called on more than ever to perform the same duties and take the same risks as active-duty members, reserve and active-duty professions differ in a number of ways.

The most important difference may be that reservists can have a civilian career while employed in the Reserves. This allows them to develop civilian and firm-specific skills, contributing to their civilian earnings potential relative to active-duty members.[9] In addition, many reservists will qualify for private pension benefits through their civilian employers. While retirees from active duty may

----

[9] The return to military experience in the civilian labor market, especially for individuals with lengthy military careers, is essentially unknown. Research typically shows that active-duty retirees earn substantially less than their civilian counterparts, but it is unclear

also be covered under a civilian employer's pension plan, the reservist's higher tenure with a civilian employer will probably lead to larger pension benefits. Furthermore, frequent or long activations might disrupt a reservist's civilian career progression, as discussed further in the next subsection. In contrast, deployments may give active-duty members more hands-on, job-related experiences while contributing to their performance, their career progression, and, ultimately, their compensation.

Reserve duty when nonactivated has a relatively predictable and limited routine—a weekend of drilling each month and two weeks of training in the summer.[10] Active-duty members, in contrast, frequently must work long, irregular hours to hone their skills; maintain and repair their equipment; and prepare for inspections, exercises, training, and deployment. Many active-duty members spend days or weeks away from home for training, professional development courses, and exercises.

Active-duty members and their families are relocated every few years under permanent change of station (PCS) moves, whereas reservists are not subject to such moves. A PCS move means severing ties to friends and community and, for many members, finding new housing and changing their children's school. Active-duty families move three times as often as their civilian counterparts, and the moves are typically for longer distances. Sometimes families are stationed abroad, and other times a member is assigned abroad on an unaccompanied tour and is separated from his or her family. The pattern of frequent movement also takes a toll on the earnings potential of the military spouse. Wives of active-duty members are less likely to be employed, work fewer weeks per year when employed (in part because of family moves), and earn a lower hourly wage, all leading to lower annual earnings on average (Hosek et al., 2002). By comparison, although reservists' spouses must plan their family schedules and labor-force participation around the reserve schedule of monthly drills and annual training, they are otherwise little affected by the reservist's regimen during times of nonactivation.

---

to what degree this gap reflects unobserved characteristics of military retirees that may depress earnings. See, for example, Loughran (2001b).

[10] As mentioned, it could be argued that the computation of pro rata years of service is overly generous. A reservist receives 15 points for affiliating with a component of the Selected Reserves and a point for each drill, rather than a point for a day. A strict pro rata accounting on a day-of-service basis would eliminate the 15 points for affiliation and half of the points for drills, or approximately 24 points. If 39 points were taken away for each of, say, 10 years of reserve service, the reservist would have 390/360 = 1.08 fewer pro rata years in the computation of reserve retirement benefits.

Reservists have been activated for military operations more frequently since the end of the Cold War than during it, and activations have increased since September 11, 2001. Active and reserve data are still becoming available for the recent operations in Afghanistan and Iraq—namely, Operation Iraqi Freedom, Operation Noble Eagle, and Operation Enduring Freedom—and for the war on terrorism, so we can give only a rough idea of active versus reserve deployment at present. For actives, the percentage of first-term active-duty enlisted personnel with hostile deployment in the three-year period ending in 1999 was 27 percent in the Army, 55 percent in the Navy, 33 percent in the Air Force, and 26 percent in the Marine Corps.[11] The percentages with any deployment, whether hostile or nonhostile, was 54 for the Army, 76 for the Navy, 43 for the Air Force, and 63 for the Marine Corps. The hostile-deployment percentages have no doubt greatly increased since September 11, 2001. For the reserves, 374,130 current Selected Reserve members in August 2004 had experienced activation at some point in the 36-month period from September 11, 2001, to August 31 2004, according to information provided by the Defense Manpower Data Center (DMDC) based on its Activation Contingency File for Operations Noble Eagle, Enduring Freedom, and Iraqi Freedom. This was 40.9 percent of the Selected Reserve force. Of these activations, 142,785, or 16.7 percent of the Selected Reserve Force was still active. We do not know how many of these reservist deployments involved hostile duty.[12]

In considering the issue of equity of active and reserve duty, it may be the case that the active members are present and in service all of the time, whereas reservists are called up only "when the shooting starts" and therefore are at greater risk of injury or death. We have no data or information to draw on to support this hypothesis, but it seems relevant to the notion of equity.

---

[11] These percentages are for personnel who completed their term and faced a reenlistment decision. Personnel who left before completing their term are not counted. The percentages for second-term personnel and officers are similar. See Fricker (2002) and Hosek and Totten (2002).

[12] The Activation Contingency file is created by merging together several sources of information including the Defense Enrollment Eligibility Reporting System data, the Services' Contingency data, PERSTEMPO data, and Pay files that indicate that deployment-related pays were executed. A different source of information on mobilizations is the Services Daily Mobilization Report, provided by the Joint Staff. According to that report, there were 418,748 mobilizations as of August 2004. This figure exceeds the 374,130 figure for a variety of reasons. First, the Contingency file focuses on individuals who have been activated and excludes multiple mobilizations. Second, the Contingency file gives weekly rather than a daily report, resulting in a time lag. Third, it includes volunteers. Fourth, it may include those who received orders but failed to report. Fifth, there may be differences in the treatment in the mobilization of full-time reservists (Active Guard Reserve).

Many of the recent reserve deployments have been long, arguably much longer than reservists expected. According to testimony in March 2004 by Assistant Secretary of Defense for Reserve Affairs Thomas Hall to the Personnel Subcommittee of the Senate Committee on Armed Services, for those reservists who have completed their tours of duty in the current contingencies in Operations Noble Eagle, Enduring Freedom, and Iraqi Freedom, tour lengths averaged 320 days. Absences of close to a year are hard on families (whether active or reserve) and may affect a reservist's civilian career. Despite legal protection to ensure that an activated reservist will be held harmless with respect to job security, pay, and advancement opportunities,[13] such protection may be difficult to implement in practice. On the other hand, analysis of the earnings of activated reservists in 2002 and 2003 relative to 2000 indicates that average earnings increased relative to what earnings would have been had reservists not been activated (Loughran, Klerman, and Martin, 2006). Reservists who served 30 or fewer active days in 2000 and more than 30 days in 2002 and 2003, experienced a net gain of 22 percent over their base year earnings of $42,235 in 2000. Though average earnings increased with active duty days, some reservists do experience an earnings loss when activated. Loughran, Klerman, and Martin estimated that 17 percent of those who were activated more than 30 days in 2002 or 2003 experienced a loss, with 6 percent experiencing a loss of more than $10,000. Interestingly, an even larger fraction of reservists who were not activated experienced an earnings loss. Thus, 40 percent of reservists who were not activated in 2002 or 2003 experienced an earnings loss. Thus, activation reduced the likelihood of experiencing an earnings loss, on average, in those years. Perhaps employers will be less willing to place reservists in positions of responsibility, where a lengthy absence would be harmful to the company, or to make up the difference between reserve pay and pay on the job.

As this discussion has shown, there are different demands placed on active and reserve components. Whether these demands have become more equal as a result of the increased deployment of reservists is an empirical question that can be answered only by considering a number of factors. Actives and reservists alike signed up to serve, and today's

---

[13] The Uniformed Services Employment and Reemployment Rights Act was passed in October 1994 and revised in 1996 and 1998. The nonprofit organization Employer Support for the Guard and Reserve (ESGR) provides information to employers about the act. According to ESGR, the act "seeks to ensure that members of the uniformed services are entitled to return to their civilian employment upon completion of their service. They should be reinstated with the seniority, status, and rate of pay they would have obtained had they remained continuously employed by their civilian employer. The law also protects individuals from

more frequent and lengthy deployments may be both more fulfilling and more burdensome simultaneously. Lengthy absences, often accompanied by uncertainty or abrupt changes in the date of departure and the date of return, may create more family stress than the previous pattern of less frequent deployment. But in the case of reservists, the increased deployment may be disruptive to their civilian careers and earnings, whereas for actives there may be little disruption.[14] The reservist's absence may also adversely affect his or her employer, which might affect the employer's implicit policy on hiring, training, advancing, and placing reservists in positions of responsibility. In other words, the employer's eventual response to the reservist's more frequent, longer deployment might result in a further negative effect on the reservist. On the other hand, activation for reservists has proven lucratvive on average, though some reservists have experienced an earnings loss.

A different perspective about equity is gained by recognizing the simple fact that individuals freely chose between civilian, active-duty, and reserve careers knowing that the three choices entail differences in compensation, including retirement pay. This brings us to another facet of equity, which is competitiveness. In a competitive market, individuals are wage-takers and choose jobs that maximize utility. Likewise, a competitive market demands that employers offer wages that minimize costs. The result is that individuals are paid their marginal product. If they do not like the pay or other characteristics of their job, then they are free to leave and seek a job with more amenable characteristics. This is the basic environment in which the military must operate. They must offer individuals a bundle of job characteristics, including retirement benefits, that attracts and motivates the individuals they wish to attract and motivate. Efficiency demands that they offer no more than this. Thus, if we assume a competitive market, then, in equilibrium, reservists receive less retirement pay than active-duty members because they are willing to accept less retirement pay, either because the nature of the reserve job differs or because their outside opportunities differ.

Insofar as reservists now face unexpectedly higher risks of long deployment and choose to leave at a higher rate, efficiency demands that compensation for reservists should rise to maintain personnel force size. However, that rise in compensation can come in many forms, such as

discrimination in hiring, promotion, and retention on the basis of present and future membership in the armed services" (ESGR, 2004).
[14] Frequent deployment can disrupt training schedules, attending schools required for promotion, and access to firing ranges needed to stay qualified. However, evidence from deployments in the 1990s indicates that they did not delay promotions (Hosek and Totten, 2002).

higher basic pay or higher bonuses and special pay. It need not come in the form of more generous retirement benefits. An equitable or fair retirement system in this view is a retirement system that, along with other forms of compensation, results in a force with desirable characteristics, without either the actives or the reservists being paid less or more than needed to achieve this force.

Recognition of More Frequent and Longer Deployments

The increased use of reserve forces in peacetime operations, small-scale contingencies, and the war on terrorism may be changing the way reservists think about the adequacy of reserve compensation relative to the obligations of serving as a reservist. Reservists know the Reserves are part of the total force and so are at risk of activation and deployment. But the war on terrorism and the operations in Afghanistan and Iraq are challenging the validity of past expectations about the frequency and length of deployment. According to Army Reserve Chief Lt. General James Helmly, reservists were being advised in 2004 to expect a 9- to 12-month activation every 4 to 5 years, rather than every 8 to 9 years (Loeb, 2004). This nearly doubled a reservist's expected time away from home. The increase for the actives may be as great. For instance, active-duty personnel have been rotated to the Middle East, to overseas bases (Okinawa or Germany), and again to the Middle East. The number of personnel deployed to Iraq and Afghanistan should decline as the process of nation building progresses, but the situations in Bosnia and Kosovo imply the need for a sizeable ground-force presence for some years.

The high current pace of deployment and heightened expectation of future deployments threaten to reduce reserve retention and recruitment and therefore may require changes in personnel force management and compensation. Would a change in reserve retirement benefits, such as lowering the age of benefit receipt from 60 to 55, be a helpful response? We have argued that it would be a weak response because of personal discounting and the fact that many reservists will never qualify for retirement benefits. It is also weak because it is not targeted to personnel who actually deploy. In that sense, it is like an across-the-board increase in compensation rather than a deployment-contingent increase. An across-the-board increase gives somewhat higher pay to everyone to address the higher risk of deployment that all face. A deployment-contingent increase offers an assurance to each reservist that, if and when deployment occurs, deployment-related pay would compensate for the burden of that deployment. A deployment-contingent system is flexible in the sense that it scales up as deployments increase and scales down when they decrease.

We do not have a theory of how much of a pay increase should be across-the-board and how much deployment-contingent, but it is useful to recognize that deployment imposes some costs on members and their families, as discussed above.[15] As a result, deployment-contingent pay is well targeted for offsetting these costs. Leading examples of deployment-related pay are family separation pay, imminent danger pay, certain places pay, and combat zone tax exclusion.

With respect to the effect of deployments on retention, Hosek and Totten (2002) found that deployments involving hostile duty have a small positive effect on active-duty reenlistment for first-term personnel and a larger positive effect for second-term personnel. Reenlistment tended to decline as deployment lengthened; even so, reenlistment was typically higher for members who deployed than for those who did not. Fricker (2002) found that hostile deployment has little effect on officer continuation. Hosek and Totten (1998, 2002) emphasize the role of the member's expectations about deployment—the expected frequency of deployment, the expected length of deployment, and the expected variance in frequency and length. Members seek to join the service and occupational area where the expected pattern of deployment most closely aligns with their preferences for deployment. When deployment actually occurs, substantial deviations in its frequency and length from what the member expects may be dissatisfying and can cause the member to revise his or her expectations about deployment, which in turn can affect the member's willingness to reenlist.

Like reservists, employers may also have expectations about how often and how long their reservist employees will be deployed. Employers may be willing to support activated reservists for some range of deployment, in terms of preserving their career opportunity or replacing lost pay, but may be unwilling to do so if the call-ups become frequent and long. An implication of the fact that employers may bear a cost of deployment is that they will respond to minimize or avoid this cost.

Deployment-contingent pay responds to the fact that deployment frequency and length are not shared evenly among reservists, as we show next. Table 2.1 contains the number of reservists where were serving August 2004 who had ever been activated for the Operation Noble Eagle in Afghanistan and Operations Enduring Freedom and Iraqi Freedom in Iraq, based on information provided by the DMDC based on their Activation-

---

[15] Deployment also creates some intrinsic benefits. Members often find deployment itself to be satisfying. It is a time of intense activity when training and experience can be put to use, and members may gain

Contingency File. Table 2.2 presents the average completed tour length of these reservists for these operations, by component. For all components, the total number of reservists in August 2004 who had ever been activated was 374,130, representing 40.9 percent of the August 2004 Selected Reserve end-strength. Of these individuals, 16.7 percent were still active, while the remaining had been deactivated. Many, around 56,000, had been deployed more than once. The average duration for those who had completed a tour was 295 days for all components, or over three-quarters of a year, far in excess of the usual "two days a month, two weeks in the summer" expectation of reserve service if one is not activated.

Table 2.1

Selected Reservists who Have Been Activated for Operations Noble Eagle, Enduring Freedom, and Iraqi Freedom as of August 31, 2004; Selected Reserve End-strength August 2004

Reserve Component	Total Still Active	Deactivated Since 9/11	Total Deployed	End-Strength
Army Guard	80,686	74,272	154,958	342,130
U.S. Army			80,387	206,775
Reserve	30,791	49,596		
US Coast				
Guard				
Reserve	1,713	4,803	6,516	7,918
Air Guard	7,458	39,634	47,092	106,687
U.S Air				
Force				
Reserve	6,720	23,480	30,200	74,794
U.S.				
Marine				
Corps			30,933	40,020
Reserve	11,082	19,851		
U.S. Navy				
Reserve	4,335	19,709	24,044	82,440
Total	142,785	231,345	374,130	852,846

satisfaction from serving their country, interacting with their unit members, and helping the local people.

Table 2.2

**Average Completed Tour Length for Selected Reservists Activated for
Operations Noble Eagle, Enduring Freedom, and Iraqi Freedom, as of
August 31, 2004**

Reserve Component	Total	Average Days Activated
Army Guard	74,272	337.1
U.S. Army Reserve	49,596	330.2
US Coast Guard Reserve	4,803	256.1
Air Guard	39,634	231.5
U.S Air Force Reserve	23,480	312.1
U.S. Marine Corps Reserve	19,851	237.8
U.S. Navy Reserve	19,709	277.5
Total	231,345	299.7

Note: Population includes only those who are no longer active as of
August 31, 2004
SOURCE: DMDC, Activation Contingency File.

Analyses of activations by DMDC show that specific occupational
groups and components have a disproportionate burden of call-up. For
example, civil affairs personnel such as those in law enforcement,
pilots, and those in motor vehicle operations, intelligence and
communications have experienced more frequent deployments. As shown in
Table 2.1, deployments have also fallen disproportionately on the Marine
Corps Reserve, Coast Guard Reserve, and Army Guard. The Army Guard
accounts for over half of those still active at that time
(80,686/142,785) but only about 40 percent (342,130/852,846) of
Selected Reserve end-strength. Those serving in the Army Guard also have
had longer activations, on average, as shown in Table 2.2.

There is also evidence to suggest that deployments have not
affected reservists equally in the past. We have data on the
distribution of annual retirement point accumulations for the years
1987, 1991, 1995, and 1999. Retirement point accumulations are related
to days of service and provide an indication of whether past deployments
affected only a small fraction of reservists. We plot these annual
retirement point accumulations for officers and enlisted personnel by
decile and year in Figure 2.2.

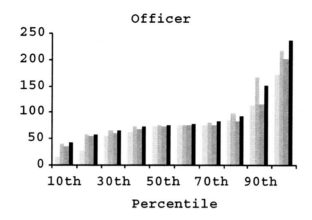

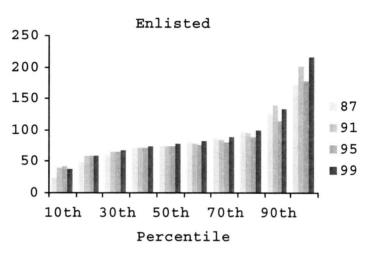

Figure 2.2—Annual Retirement Point Accumulations for Officer and
Enlisted Personnel by Decile: 1987, 1991, 1995, 1999

As seen, annual point accumulations in the middle of the
distribution barely changed over the period from 1987 to 1999. During
the Gulf War in 1991 some 250,000 reservists were mobilized, and the
effect of this is seen in the tails of the distribution—the average
number of points in the highest decile increased by about 25 points.
Between 1995 and 1996, reserve man-days increased from 8 million to 13.5
million (excluding Desert Shield/Desert Storm), and man-days stood at
12.5 million in 1999. The effect of this increase in man-days on point
accumulations also is concentrated in the upper tail of the
distribution. For officers, point accumulations at the ninetieth
percentile increased from 114 to 134 points and at the ninety-fifth
percentile from 177 to 216. For enlisted members, these point increases

_____

[16] The median point accumulation increased by only 3 points for both
officers and enlisted personnel between 1987 and 1999. This increase

were from 117 to 151 and from 201 to 237, respectively. At the seventieth and eightieth percentiles, point accumulations increased by about 10 points from a base of about 75 or 80 points. This could reflect actual increases in deployments or the relaxing of the inactive-duty point cap.

Thus, despite the large number of deployments, a sizable majority of reservists were not mobilized in the past. As a result, a reserve compensation system that compensated for a greater anticipated burden of deployment by increasing the pay of every reservist would not be fair or efficient. It would not be fair because, as deployments are actually realized, some reservists will have many more deployments than others. It would not be efficient because the length and conditions of deployment, and hence the psychic and monetary costs of deployment, might differ widely among members and not be adequately compensated by the average amount on which a uniform increase in compensation would be premised. By implication, an increase in retirement benefits that affects all personnel is unlikely to be the best way to recognize and compensate members who are now experiencing, and may expect in the future, a high burden of deployment.

Ensuring an Adequate Supply of Reservists

Past studies of military recruiting and retention find that military compensation, including basic pay, bonuses, allowances, and retirement benefits, powerfully influences whether the armed forces can recruit and retain sufficient numbers of qualified personnel with the right mix of skills and experience. Retirement benefits play two key roles within the context of the goals of military compensation: first, to help members provide for old age; second, to affect the shape of the personnel force structure with respect to the distribution of personnel by rank and year of service. The military achieves the latter by providing retention and separation incentives to personnel at different ages, ranks, and YOS. This is clearly what legislators had in mind when they established the reserve retirement system in 1948 as part of the Army and Air Force Vitalization and Retirement Equalization Act. The Committee on Armed Services in the House of Representatives detailed the purpose of reserve retirement as follows:

> The underlying purpose in writing this policy as to reserve components into law is that the retirement benefit will furnish an incentive that will hold men in the reserve components for a longer period of time. It was stressed by practically every witness who testified on this feature of the bill that the most desirable type of Reserve was a reserve of men with accumulated

---

probably reflects the relaxing of the inactive-duty point cap from 60 to 75 points in September 1996.

training. It was also pointed out that the direct monetary emoluments payable to the Reserve officers and men were so small that in many instances as the men grew older, became married, and took on family obligations, unless an additional incentive were offered them, they would drop their reserve training.[17]

Thus, another critical aspect of assessing reserve retirement reforms is their effect on recruitment and retention.

Why do individuals choose to stay and eventually retire from the Reserves, and how do compensation policies affect this choice? These questions have been analyzed for active-duty personnel using an economic model known as the dynamic retention model (DRM), which assumes individuals consider the current returns and option value of staying and choose to stay if the sum of these values is larger than the value of being solely in the civilian sector. As part of our larger project, we have extended the DRM to incorporate the affiliation and retention decisions of reservists (Asch, Hosek, Clendenning, and Mattock, 2003). In the broader model, the active member is assumed to choose each period whether to stay on active duty or to leave and affiliate with a reserve component, or leave to active duty and not affiliate. One of the advantages of extending the DRM to incorporate both active and reserve decision making is to analyze how reserve compensation policies such as changes in the reserve retirement system can affect active-duty retention and the transition from the actives to the Reserves. Our larger project is investigating these issues.

In the extended model, the net payoff to participating in the Reserves depends on how long an individual plans to stay in the Reserves and whether the individual might choose to return to the Reserves after leaving. That is, the payoff depends on the career path the individual follows. We hypothesize that when deciding whether to join the Reserves, whether to stay, and whether to leave and reenter at a later date, individuals evaluate the payoffs to all possible career paths that they might follow and weigh each path by the probability that they will follow it. Career paths are dimensioned by years of reserve service, years of active service, and years of civilian experience (exclusive of reserve service). Since those with stronger tastes for reserve service will have longer careers in the reserve components, such individuals will place more weight on payoffs associated with such careers in the Reserves including retirement benefits. In contrast, individuals with a weaker taste for reserve service will be less likely to serve until they qualify for retirement benefits and will put more weight on payoffs occurring in the near term.

---

[17] U.S. House of Representatives (80th Congress, 1947), House Report 816, as quoted in U.S. DoD (1988).

Aside from tastes, the decision to join, stay, or rejoin the Reserves also depends on the level of reserve pay and its growth over one's career from promotion and longevity increases as well as annual basic-pay increases, the transferability and value of training in civilian jobs, the level and type of educational benefits, and special and incentive pay such as reenlistment bonuses. As discussed above, the decision also depends on prevalence and duration of deployments.

The value of leaving the Reserves depends on civilian opportunities with and without reserve participation. Civilian opportunities might be higher in the absence of reserve participation because more time can be spent pursuing other activities, and travel costs and other expenses associated with drilling can be avoided. All else being equal, the better the civilian opportunities are without reserve participation, the less likely an individual will continue to serve.

Another factor affecting the reserve retention decision is the rate at which personnel discount future income. Here, it is useful to distinguish between the rate of time preference and the rate of interest. The rate of time preference reflects the rate at which the individual is willing to exchange consumption in period t for consumption in period $t + 1$. The rate of time preference is also called the *personal discount rate*. The rate of interest reflects the rate at which the individual can transfer wealth from one period to the next, for example, by borrowing or lending. Past research indicates that personnel have personal discount rates in excess of 10 percent (Warner and Pleeter, 2001). On theoretical grounds, if an individual's consumption level is equal from one period to the next, then in equilibrium the personal discount rate is equal to the interest rate. More specifically, the willingness to trade consumption between periods is represented by the ratio of the marginal utility of consumption in $t + 1$ to the marginal utility of consumption in t. When the level of consumption is the same in the two periods, the ratio of marginal utilities is by definition equal to one plus the personal discount rate.

---

[18] We thank Nicole Maestas for encouraging us to clarify the distinction between the rate of time preference and the interest rate.

[19] Discount rates vary with age, with younger personnel discounting future pay and benefits at very high rates. Discount rates also vary with education with better-educated personnel discounting future pay and benefits at lower rates. Warner and Pleeter (2001) estimate personal discount rates for military members of 0 to over 30 percent with the low rates corresponding to senior officers and the high rates corresponding to junior enlisted personnel. Estimated private discount rates between 15 and 20 percent are not uncommon in the economics literature. In contrast, DoD's Office of the Actuary discounts future retirement liabilities at a rate of 6.5 percent. This is a nominal rate. The real

The rate at which wealth can be transferred from t to $t + 1$ is equal to one plus the interest rate. So when consumption is equal in the two periods, it follows that the personal discount rate equals the interest rate.

As a result, the empirical finding of high personal discount rates is cause to believe that interest rates are also high.[20] In particular, the interest rates faced by military personnel may be considerably higher than the interest rate faced by the government. High interest rates reduce the value of future pay relative to current pay. At a 10 percent interest rate, the present value of $1 is $.62 if paid 5 years from now, $.39 if paid 10 years from now, and $.15 if paid 20 years from now.

Ability or aptitude has an ambiguous effect on the retention decision. More capable individuals may be more or less likely to stay in the Reserves than less capable individuals, depending on how ability and aptitude are rewarded in the civilian market relative to the military's "internal" market. The internal reward to ability depends in part on the extent to which the promotion system identifies and promotes the more capable more rapidly and with higher probability.

Finally, the model recognizes that the future is not perfectly knowable, and random factors affect the payoff of remaining in the Reserves. Such factors might be an unexpected improvement in the local civilian labor market, or a desirable assignment. Each year individuals experience new random shocks to the payoff to staying in the active components and to staying in the Reserves. A key feature of the DRM is the idea that individuals make retention decisions at each age with uncertainty about future payoffs, and the model handles this uncertainty by assuming the individual will make the optimal choice in the future given the shocks that occur then. Because the shocks are not knowable beforehand, the best the individual can do today is to take the expected value of future outcomes, knowing that future decisions will be the best under the circumstances. The model represents this behavior by taking the expected value of the maximum of the random payoffs in each future period.

---

rate equals this rate minus the rate of inflation (presumably the long-term expected rate of inflation).

[20] We prefer this somewhat loose wording for two reasons. Consumption will not be exactly equal from one period to the next, although, frankly, we do not expect it to be much different. Furthermore, military personnel do not have full control of their consumption decisions. This is especially evident when personnel are deployed. The lack of control over consumption while in the military may help resolve the puzzle of why the personal discount rates found by Warner and Pleeter appear far higher than the interest rates likely to be available to personnel. An extension of the usual model that built in restrictions on consumption behavior would be required to analyze this conjecture.

The Effects of Reserve Retirement on Retention

The DRM provides a framework for evaluating the incentive effects of the reserve retirement system. Perhaps the strongest incentive created by reserve retirement is the incentive to earn 20 creditable YOS. The cliff vesting provision of reserve retirement implies a large increase in the value or payoff associated with leaving the Reserves at the age at which the reservist reaches the twentieth year of creditable service. All else being equal, cliff vesting increases the probability that for any given reservist the value of separating will be maximized at some point at or after, not before, the twentieth year. As a result, the reserve retirement system creates a strong incentive to remain in the Reserves until at least 20 YCS have been attained. Of course, some individuals will depart prior to that point, or never enlist at all, because of the inconveniences associated with reserve service, distaste for military service generally, the possibility of receiving higher civilian earnings if not a member of the Reserves, or some other, potentially random, factor that diminishes the utility of reserve service.

The effect of cliff vesting at 20 YOS can be seen in reserve retention and separation profiles. In Figure 2.3, continuation rates at each YOS in the Reserves gradually rise from around 70 to 80 percent among reservists with one to five YOS to around 95 percent among reservists with 15-19 YOS. The continuation rate falls sharply at 20 YOS; 73 percent of enlisted reservists and 83 percent of reserve officers with 20 YOS continue in that year. The continuation rate initially rises from its low point at 20 YOS and then begins to fall again through 30 plus YOS. That prospective retirement benefits weigh more heavily on retention decisions as YCS increase (prior to 20 years) is reflected in data from the 1986 Reserve Components Survey (RCS). Whereas about 30 percent of members with one to five YOS reported that retirement benefits played a major role in their most recent reenlistment decision, this percentage increased to over 70 percent of members with 12-19 YCS (U.S. DoD, 1988).[21]

---

[21] To some extent this pattern in the data also reflects the fact that reservists who remain to 12-19 years of service have selected to do so and so most likely place a higher value on retirement benefits than the entirety of their entering cohort.

Figure 2.3—Reserve Annual Continuation Rates by YOS, 1999-2000

This brings us to another important incentive effect of reserve retirement: the incentive it creates for individuals to self-sort according to ability (Asch and Warner, 1994). Importantly, the prospect of becoming vested in retirement benefits at 20 YCS will, all else being equal, have a greater retention effect on individuals who place a high probability of remaining in the Reserves until 20 YCS than those who do not. The probability of remaining in the Reserves, in turn, is in part a function of promotion prospects. On average, high-ability individuals will tend to advance faster than low-ability individuals and so are less likely to be subject to mandatory separation due to years-in-grade ("up-or-out") restrictions. In addition, their faster rate of promotion means the value of their retirement benefits will be greater since retirement pay is a function of pay grade. Thus, vesting at 20 YCS will provide a greater carrot for high-ability individuals because they are less likely to be forced out and because the value of retirement benefits increases with pay.

This is precisely the type of self-sorting the military wishes to encourage. The military fills its upper echelons with individuals who move up through the ranks; there is no lateral entry into high ranks. Consequently, military compensation should encourage high-ability individuals to stay and seek promotion. At the same time, the military

---

[22] A full treatment of promotion in the Selected Reserves extends beyond this brief discussion. It is commonly thought that promotion in the Reserves often requires finding a job at a higher rank in local units because there may be no immediate opening in one's own unit. Changing units may disrupt friendships and increase or decrease travel expenses. The gains from promotion in the form of greater responsibility, greater authority, higher pay, and higher expected retirement benefits are all incentives that encourage a reservist to seek promotion despite the "transactions costs" of doing so.

wants to encourage low-ability individuals to separate relatively early in their careers without necessarily forcing them to do so. Involuntary separation, while legal, has potentially high costs by adversely affecting morale—individuals may perceive the prospect of involuntary separation as risky and unfair—and encouraging individuals to lobby against the policy (Milgrom, 1988).

Although the compensation structure offers greater incentives to high-ability individuals to stay and seek higher rank, they might also have better civilian prospects for earnings and advancement. Therefore, although embedding a good incentive structure in military compensation is crucial to quality retention and sorting, the effectiveness of the incentive structure will depend on how well it measures up to outside alternatives. Large organizations, for example, also have incentive structures to keep and sort high-ability employees. As a result, the overall effectiveness of the military incentive structure depends not only on the sorting incentives but also on the retention incentives (the military must pay enough to induce the high-ability individuals to stay). The amount the military must pay for retention depends on the correlation between ability and taste for military service. The military will be able to set a lower pay scale if ability and taste are positively correlated than if they are negatively correlated. But even if the correlation were zero, the military would still have to set compensation high enough to keep high-ability personnel. This could result in "overpaying" low-ability personnel if all pay were current and none deferred. Yet an advantage of the military promotion system, which favors the retention and sorting of high-ability personnel, is that pay at lower grades can be the same for both high- and low-ability personnel, but the value of the military career will be higher for high-ability personnel. This allows the military to avoid overpaying junior low-ability personnel in its desire to keep junior high-ability personnel.

Beyond encouraging self-sorting by ability, the structure of retirement benefits encourages all individuals to exert effort by seeking promotion (Asch and Warner, 1994). Because the value of retirement pay increases with rank and years of satisfactory service, promotion is rewarded not only by an increase in current compensation but also by an increase in future compensation in terms of higher retirement pay and the chance to reach still higher grades, which would raise retirement pay still further.

Reserve Retirement and Force-Shaping in Today's Reserves

Because the reserve retirement system was designed in a different era, it is natural to ask whether the incentives it creates are desirable given the environment in which the Reserves operate today. The sixth QRMC focused on reserve compensation and on retirement specifically. It indicated in its final report that maintaining an incentive to serve through 20 YOS should be a basic feature of any reserve retirement system. Deferring a portion of compensation by means of retirement vesting at 20 YOS creates an incentive for trained individuals to remain in the Reserves at least to that point, thereby increasing the return on the considerable investment made by the Reserves to train and develop its force.

The sixth QRMC and others did express concern, however, about the relatively weak incentives of the current reserve retirement system to separate voluntarily after 20 YOS.[23] On the active-duty side, it is clear that legislators desired a retirement system that helped maintain a young and vigorous active-duty force. Making retirement benefits payable immediately upon retirement is an inducement for older personnel to leave. At the time of vesting, active-duty members weigh the benefits of separating and accepting an immediate annuity today against the benefits of additional service, a possibly higher rank, and higher retirement benefits because of additional YOS and the possibly higher rank. Since YOS have a relatively small impact on the value of the annuity and the prospect of further advancement may be low for many members, the financial value of remaining on active duty increases comparatively little after 20 YOS relative to the years leading up to 20 years. For active-duty members with sufficiently high discount rates or subjective mortality risk, the present discounted value of retirement benefits could actually fall in value with additional YOS. Also, for active-duty members, starting a second career is an incentive to leave.

For reservists, on the other hand, continued service after 20 years can only add to the value of their retirement benefits at age 60 since they do not forgo retirement pay by serving an additional year, and they do not need to start a second career. Relative to the active-duty system, then, reserve retirement provides little incentive to separate after 20 YOS.

At the time of the sixth QRMC, the reserve components complained that their force structures were more heavily concentrated in later YOS than desired. They wanted more members with 6 to 20 YOS and fewer with 25 to 30 YOS (DoD, 1988), and they attributed this imbalance in part to the absence of an immediate annuity in the reserve retirement system.

---

[23] There is little in the legislative history to suggest why age 60 was chosen as the age of pension receipt for reservists. The fifth edition of the *Military Compensation Background Papers* (U.S. DoD, 1996) speculates that age 60 was chosen because this was the minimum age at which federal civil service employees could voluntarily retire at that time.

The apparent reasoning was that, given a fixed hierarchy, higher senior separation increases the number of senior positions available and so increases the probability that any mid-career member will be promoted. Mid-career reservists who might otherwise have left would stay and seek promotion, encouraged by the higher chance of promotion. In fact, since the sixth QRMC, the number of months in grade has increased in the Reserves among mid-career members. Whether this is due to higher senior retention or a decreased inflow to mid-career ranks is unknown. Also, YOS and age have increased in the Reserves. Relative to the active-duty force, reservists are older and have more YOS.

Despite the concerns voiced by the reserve components at the time of the sixth QRMC, it is not clear whether the increases since then in time in grade, average YOS, and average age pose a problem. Studies have found that the productivity of military personnel increases with their experience, although these studies focus on junior personnel rather than senior personnel and so might not be a good guide to the gains from greater seniority in the Reserves. Similarly, we do not know empirically how many mid-career reservists were deterred from staying because of a lower probability of promotion; indeed, we do not know whether the increase in senior time in grade resulted from a reduced outflow, a reduced inflow (fewer promotions from the mid-career ranks), or both. Without empirical knowledge of the gains from greater seniority and the reasons for the increase in seniority, it is difficult to judge the potential benefits of these changes against the cost of a more senior force.

In the same vein, we do not know how the reserve components set their retention goals. The goals may or may not reflect a component's ongoing critical assessment of its manpower requirements given changing missions and technology. Also, it may be that the Reserves could achieve its retention goals at lower cost with changes in its compensation system, including the retirement system. Research on the active-duty force indicates the feasibility of maintaining the same retention profile, increasing incentives for effort related to promotion, and lowering the total cost of compensation by changes that reduce deferred compensation and increase current compensation.[24] The Reserves are different than the actives, and the reserve retirement benefit system defers much less compensation than does the active-duty system (this is implied by Figure 2.1). A separate analysis would be required to determine whether similar changes in the structure of reserve compensation would be cost-effective.

---

[24] Estimates of cost savings depend crucially on the assumed value of the government discount rate (see Asch, Johnson, and Warner, 1998).

As with the actives, the structure of compensation exerts a major influence on the reserve personnel force structure. Changing the structure of compensation can be expected, over time, to change the personnel force structure. Consequently, it is not only useful to ask how a given change in reserve retirement benefits would affect retention and personnel force structure and how much it would cost, but also whether the personnel force structure is being improved. With available data and models, it is easier to determine how personnel force structure will change, although this is not simple, than to determine whether the change is an improvement. Put differently, changing the reserve retirement benefit structure should not be done merely because it can be done, or only because it responds to concerns about perceived inequity, but also because such change is in the interest of national security.

Flexible Personnel Management

The reserve components employ individuals with a wide range of skills. While it may be desirable to create broad incentives for individuals to complete long reserve careers, these incentives should not interfere with the components' ability to pursue personnel management objectives in specific skill areas. Cliff vesting at 20 YOS, for example, creates an incentive to serve through 20 YOS but also makes it difficult for personnel managers to separate personnel nearing 20 years. Personnel managers may be reluctant to separate mid-careerists because of the large financial penalty for the separated individual and may be concerned that some would view their action as favoritism (keeping personnel they like, separating those not liked). As a result, the components may keep more mid-careerists than they otherwise would in the absence of cliff vesting *and* an objective, rule-based, fair means of separating mid-careerists.

The components may also find it difficult to involuntarily separate individuals with more than 20 YOS. Involuntary separation deprives the reservist of a position he or she has earned and wants to be in. In addition, reservists who serve long careers may come to rely on their reserve income, income that might be difficult to replace through other work. Personnel managers may be reluctant to separate individuals with more than 20 YOS when they cannot offer any separation pay to offset the loss of current reserve income. This is also true for separating mid-careerists, although in their case the loss is current reserve income plus the present value of expected future retirement benefits.

Given the diversity of roles and missions in the total force, components may desire different retention profiles. Within a component, it may be desirable to generate different retention profiles for different occupations, for example, long careers for legal professionals, pilots, procurement specialists, and short careers in specialties that demand youth and vigor. In this regard, one goal of retirement reform should be to promote flexibility in personnel management decisions. An alternative reserve retirement system should be sensitive to the prospective gains to the Reserves from encouraging different career lengths in different occupations and skill areas. Differences in career length should be based on personnel requirements and derived from a process that analyzes different experience and quality mixes before deciding on a particular mix.

Future changes in force structures from military transformation could affect the usefulness of retirement benefits as an incentive. According to the 2002 Review of the Reserve Component Contributions to National Defense, transformation is intended to expand the capability and flexibility of the total force by taking better advantage of the civilian and military expertise of current reserve members. The Review proposed that the components could flexibly access these skills by adopting a "continuum of service" approach that would allow reservists to serve in a variety of capacities from 0 to 365 days per year as needed (Office of the Assistant Secretary of Defense for Reserve Affairs,). The continuum-of-service concept is a departure from the traditional approach to reserve affiliation. If most of the reservists who would serve under the continuum-of-service concept are unlikely to reach 20 YCS, then changes in the reserve retirement benefit system will have little effect on them. The supply of individuals willing to serve under the continuum of service will depend on how current military pay compares with the cost to them of forgoing civilian opportunities including employment, schooling, or time with their families.

Cost-Effectiveness

Reforming the reserve retirement system need not lead to higher costs in the long run. As we discuss in the next section, it is possible to design alternative systems that increase the present value of retirement pay from the retiree's perspective while keeping it actuarially neutral from the government's perspective. This is because personal interest rates are likely to be substantially higher than the government interest rate.

The differential between personal interest rates and the federal (or the Actuary) rate has important implications for designing a cost-effective military compensation system. According to the 2000 RCS, over 60 percent of reserve component personnel are under age 30. Younger individuals discount future retirement benefits at a higher rate. Consequently, retirement benefits have little value relative to current pay to a large portion of reservists. From an efficiency standpoint, it is more cost-effective to front-load compensation in the form of pay, and only back-load compensation in the form of retirement benefits if doing so has beneficial force-shaping and sorting implications.

Ultimately, the cost of an alternative retirement benefit system is best understood relative to its benefits. If it is essential that the Reserves achieve some alternative accession or retention profile, then higher retirement costs may be justifiable. Economic efficiency argues that the marginal benefits of a retirement system equal its marginal costs. Efficiency also argues that for a given marginal benefit, retirement benefits should be increased only if the marginal cost of doing so is no higher than the marginal cost of increasing compensation in some other way, for example, increasing current compensation in some way. Achieving the balance between costs and benefits, of course, is difficult given the uncertainty surrounding their values. At a minimum, though, a reserve retirement system should help minimize the cost of achieving personnel management objectives.

CHAPTER THREE: CONGRESSIONAL RETIREMENT REFORM PROPOSALS

Four recent congressional bills have proposed reducing the age at which reservists may begin claiming retirement benefits, with two of the bills recommending the same proposals, one originating in the House and the other in the Senate. This section discusses the force shaping or accession and retention effects of the reform alternatives as well as their implications for management flexibility, cost, deployment, and equity.

Using the underlying theory of the stay-leave choice provided by the DRM (described in Chapter Two), we can make preliminary statements about the likely direction of retention effects of various reform proposals. Our cost estimates should also be treated as preliminary. Our research project is still under way, and it should provide the capability to simulate the retention effects and costs of various reserve retirement reform proposals.

Force-Shaping Effects

The three reform proposals included in the four bills would increase the overall value of reserve retirement benefits by changing the timing of the receipt of benefits. The immediate annuity alternative assumes that reservists would begin receiving retirement pay upon separating from the Ready Reserve as calculated under the high-three averaging system. No other parameters of the retirement system would change, like vesting at 20 YOS and cost-of-living adjustments. We assume, for simplicity, that reservists would not have a choice between high-three averaging and REDUX as do active-duty members. The age-55 alternative assumes reservists begin receiving retirement pay as calculated under high-three averaging at age 55. We also ignore other aspects of the proposals, such as TRICARE for Life. The discussion draws from the DRM model to highlight the likely effects on retention and recruiting of the increased value of retirement benefits under the three proposals.

For those with less than 20 YOS, increasing the present discounted value of reserve retirement will increase the reward for remaining in the Reserves until the 20-year vesting point. Table 3.1 shows the average present value of retirement benefits under the current system and the three alternatives for a reservist vested in the reserve retirement system using personnel data from the 1999 RCCPDS and the 2004 pay table.[25] Our estimates imply that, at a discount rate of 10 percent, an immediate annuity increases the present value of reserve retirement by 131 percent on average for the typical reservist. The age-55 and sliding-age alternatives increase the present value by 50 and 18 percent, respectively. As noted earlier, the value of a given increase in retirement benefits depends on the personal interest rate used. For a given grade, YOS, and point accumulation, younger personnel will place relatively less value on the improvements in reserve retirement proposed by Congress, because they both discount for more years and do so at a higher rate.

The DRM of reserve retention predicts that increasing the value of reserve retirement will increase reserve retention prior to 20 YOS. While we do not have estimates of the retention effects, it is clear that the magnitude of the effects generally will be small. For those close to the 20-year vesting point, annual reserve continuation rates are already quite high, as shown in Figure 2.3 in the previous section. For example, among enlisted personnel with 15 YOS, the continuation rate in FY2000 was 94 percent for enlisted reservists, which compares with 68 percent among those with 5 YOS. The high continuation rate among these mid-career personnel reflects the attraction of retirement benefits as well as the positive selection over time of personnel who are well matched with the military and have a strong taste for military service. For those with few YOS, the value of the alternatives is quite low because of young members' high interest rates and more years of discounting. A similar argument applies to the likely effect of the alternatives on accessions, especially nonprior service accessions. The value of the alternatives will be quite small to the typical nonprior service reserve recruit.

Table 3.1

Weighted Per-Capita Value of Reserve
Retirement Alternatives

Retirement System	Value
Current reserve	$45,845
Immediate annuity	$105,822
Age 55	$68,921
Sliding Age	$54,142
Actuarially neutral age-55	$56,036

SOURCE: September 1999/2000 RCCPDS.

---

[25] The average is based on the number of reservists leaving the Reserves with 20 or more YOS. At each year of service at 20 and beyond, we use the median age, modal pay grade, and median total number of points accumulated (shown in Table C-2 in Appendix C) in computing the present discounted value and present discounted cost of a retirement benefit

The DRM also predicts that the three reform alternatives will decrease retention after 20 YOS for those who have already reached the age at which they may now begin drawing benefits, for example, age 55 under one of the proposals, by lowering the net gain to staying. All three proposals reduce the age when individuals are entitled to receive benefits. The deferment of retirement among those entitled to benefits results in one less year of benefits and so makes no sense. For example, if the entitlement age is 55, a 55-year-old who does not retire and chooses to retire at age 56, forgoes benefits at age 55. The net gain to staying is reduced by these lost benefits. The incentive to leave is greater among those with more than 20 YOS and entitled to benefits, when the entitlement age is lowered, as in the three congressional alternatives.

Creating incentives for reservists in their mid-fifties to depart voluntarily after 20 or more YOS may indirectly help with mid-career retention. Given a fixed hierarchy, high senior retention lowers the number of such billets that become available each year and so lengthens time-in-grade for mid-career members. Some mid-career reservists who might otherwise stay and seek promotion become discouraged by more intense competition for a shrinking number of senior billets and separate. Conversely, by lowering senior retention, the prospects for promotion among mid-careerists improve, thereby increasing their retention. The size of this effect will depend on the number of positions actually vacated by the most senior reservists, which is a small group to begin with.

In addition, lowering the age at which retirement benefits may be received will affect the retention of reservists with 20 or more YOS but who have not yet reached the new, lower age of benefit receipt. The retention of these senior reservists will increase. By staying, they will receive longevity increases in basic pay and may be promoted. This will increase the basic-pay level that enters the computation of their retirement benefit, and because benefits will be received for more years than under the current system, the payoff to an increase in their basic pay will be greater. This provides an incentive to stay in the Reserves longer.[26]

---

alternative. We then take a weighted average, where the weights reflect the relative number of reservists separating at each year of service.

[26] There is, of course, no effect on the retention of retired reservists because they are no longer participating members of the Selected Reserves. However, a reduction in the age of benefit receipt might induce more reservists who separate with 20 or more YOS to join the retired reserve. Many already do so, however, so any increase in the rate of joining is likely to be small.

Cost

We computed the static per-capita present discounted costs of these reserve retirement reforms. Table 3.2 builds on Table 3.1 by adding a column showing costs for *new* enlisted and officer retirees assuming a real government interest rate of 2.5 percent and rate of real wage growth of 1 percent.

Table 3.2

Weighted Present Discounted Per-Capita Cost and Value of Reserve Retirement Alternatives

Retirement System	Cost	Value
Current reserve	$144,516	$45,845
Immediate annuity	$219,415	$105,822
Age 55	$179,677	$68,921
Sliding Age	$155,573	$54,142
Actuarially neutral age-55	$144,235	$56,036

SOURCE: September 1999/2000 RCCPDS.

The estimates assume that individuals will retire with the same characteristics (YOS, age, and rank) as they did in FY2000 regardless of which retirement system is in place (see Table C-2). Each entry in Table 3.2 represents a weighted average of per-capita costs for all retirees in that category. Thus, for example, the first cell reports the weighted average per-capita cost of the current retirement system ($144,516). This is substantially less than the per-capita cost under the immediate annuity and age-55 alternatives ($219,415 and $179,677). The per-capita cost of the sliding-age alternative is the least expensive of the three alternatives ($155,573), reflecting the low prevalence of new retirees below age 60 with sufficient YOS to qualify for retirement at ages below 60 on the sliding-age scale. Overall, the weighted average present discounted per-capita cost of the current system is 52 percent less than the immediate annuity alternative, 24 percent less than the age-55 alternative, and 8 percent less than the sliding-age alternative. Static cost estimates like these do not account for the retention effects of retirement reforms discussed in the previous subsection.[27]

The second column in the table shows the average present discounted per-capita value of each system assuming a 10 percent personal interest rate. These value figures are substantially lower than the cost figures. The typical retiree values retirement benefits less

---

[27] Recall that virtually all FY2000 retirees began military service prior to September 8, 1980. Their retirement pay, therefore, will be calculated using their final basic pay as opposed to high-three averaging. Thus, even the per-capita cost of the current retirement system is calculated based on retention patterns under an alternative system.

than it costs to provide them, and, depending on the personal interest rate, the difference is substantial. These figures reflect the value to reservists separating from the Reserves after completing 20 or more creditable YOS, but who have not yet reached age 60 and so are not yet drawing retirement benefits. Value would be even smaller if we considered current members who are not yet retired because we would need to discount benefits for more years (because benefits begin at a more distant age) than we do for retirees.

To further highlight the difference between value and cost, we include in the bottom row of Table 3.2 an alternative not considered in the existing legislative proposals. The new alternative would reduce the entitlement age of reserve retirement to 55, but would reduce the annuity in an actuarially neutral manner so that the average present value of per-capita cost is the same as the current system. Thus, the average per-capita cost of this alternative is $144,235, roughly equal to the current system ($144,516), by assumption. Despite the equivalence in per-capita cost, the new alternative yields a higher average per-capita value than the current system, $56,036 compared to $45,845. The greater efficiency of the actuarially fair alternative (in terms of providing more value for a given per-capita cost) stems from the difference between the government and individual interest rates. As long as individuals have a higher interest rate than the government, the present cost of providing deferred benefits will be greater than their present value to individuals. The actuarially fair alternative will not cost the government more, but it will increase federal outlays as it is phased in. That is, benefits will commence at age 55 rather than age 60. Payouts in later years, after age 60, will be somewhat lower than they would have been under the current system; the actuarially fair alternative distributes the same benefit estate over more years.

We do not attempt to project the total costs of shifting to a new reserve retirement system or how those costs might evolve over time. Such a projection is complicated by several factors. First, we do not have specific estimates of the effect of each alternative on retention rates prior to 20 YOS. We would expect the provision of early annuities to increase the number of individuals vesting in retirement at 20 YOS, an effect that would tend to increase the cost of retirement in the steady state.

Second, it is unclear how to account for reservists in the so-called gray area (between retirement and age 60) and for reservists age 60 and above who are already receiving retirement pay. Would gray-area reservists begin receiving retirement benefits according to the new system or would they be held under the current system? Would they be given a choice between systems? Would they be compensated for back retirement pay? What about reservists age 60 and over receiving retirement pay under the current system? Regardless of the answer to these questions, it is clear that simply multiplying the per-capita costs given in Table 3.2 by some projected flow of new retirees under the current system will underestimate aggregate costs of these reforms to the U.S. Treasury because of some increase in the number of reservists qualifying for retirement benefits and because of the cost of transitioning gray-area and current retirees to the new system. It also is important to note that the immediate annuity, the age-55 annuity, and the actuarially neutral age-55 alternatives would increase the total cost of future increases in basic pay.[28]

Finally, we do not account for how changes in the retirement system might affect the level of participation by reservists. For example, reducing the age of retirement benefit receipt increases the value of participation and provides members with the incentive to participate more by completing more weekend drills, performing more funeral honors duty, or completing more correspondence courses. Increases in participation will increase cost (and benefit) above what is shown in Table 3.2.

Deployment

A factor motivating the retirement reforms proposed by Congress is the increased frequency and duration of reserve deployments. There is concern that the Reserves will face a retention crisis once reservists are no longer barred from leaving while their units are mobilized in Iraq. In testimony to the Defense Subcommittee of the Senate Appropriations Committee (April 7, 2004), Lt. General James Helmly, the chief of the Army Reserve, said the concern stems from recent "open-ended" and unexpectedly long deployments.

As discussed in the previous section, the burden of deployment is not distributed equally. Therefore, reforms that affect the compensation of the entire force are unlikely to be as cost-effective as those that increase compensation contingent on deployment or more generally on the level of participation, or those that offer a mix of general and deployment-contingent compensation increases. For example, deployment pay could be increased, and the increase could be graduated so that it rose with the total amount of deployment over a given period (e.g., a

---

[28] The immediate annuity and the age-55 annuity are more generous, which alone makes them more costly. Also, the immediate annuity, the age-55 annuity, and the actuarially fair age-55 annuity are all perceived to be more generous by the reservist, which should increase retention and so increase the number of reservists qualifying for retirement benefits. Therefore, the full cost of an increase in basic pay will be greater under the alternative retirement systems than under the current system.

two-year period). In another approach, "ex ante" pay, like sea pay, could be increased for reservists with the highest risk of deployment, regardless of whether they were actually deployed. This would act as a compensating differential to recognize the greater risk of deployment associated with a given skill or occupation. But, as mentioned, this is less well targeted and hence less efficient than pay contingent on being deployed. Finally, some combination of ex ante and deployment-contingent increases could be devised.

Although the majority of reservists have not been mobilized, the expectation of deployment has increased for all reservists. Consequently, retention and accessions might be hurt even among those not directly affected by mobilization. The retirement reform alternatives proposed by Congress, which would reduce the age of entitlement, are an inefficient means of addressing this issue. The reason is that mobilization is concentrated among younger reservists, whereas the retirement reforms benefit more senior reservists, especially those in the Retired Reserve who have not yet reached age 60 but who have 20 or more YOS. Those with the greatest ex ante expectation of deployment, namely new recruits, junior, and mid-career reservists, are those who place the least value on retirement reform. Because of high personal interest rates and the large number of years over which discounting occurs, a $1 increase in retirement benefits will provide little value, compared with $1 of current compensation, for younger members and potential recruits who face the highest expectation of deployment. Although we do not have demographic data on recent call-ups, the 1992 and 2000 RCS provide data on the age distribution of reservists who experienced deployment in the 1990s and of those nearing retirement eligibility.

The first two columns of Table 3.3 show the age distributions of reservists reporting that they had been deployed in Operation Desert Storm (ODS) and those with exactly 19 YOS, drawn from the 1992 RCS. The group with 19 YOS represents those still in the Reserves and poised to achieve 20 years, and hence a group that would be a major beneficiary of the retirement reform proposals. Retired reservists would also benefit, but they are not included in the surveys. The table shows that 47 percent of those deployed for Desert Storm were ages 35 and under in 1992, while only 3 percent of those with 19 YOS were under age 35 and most likely this fraction is reporting error. Similarly, in the 2000 RCS, 43 percent of those deployed in Operation Allied Force in Kosovo were ages 35 and under, while the figure was 37 percent for those in Operation Joint Force in Bosnia.

An additional issue to consider is the potential for considerable inequity across reserve components if deployments are compensated through retirement benefits. Columns (3) and (5) in Table 3.3 show the age distribution of reserve personnel deployed during ODS who were members of the Marine Corps Reserve and the Air National Guard, while columns (4) and (6) show the distributions for all members of these components in 1992 with 19 YOS and poised to be eligible for retirement vesting eligibility. The Marine Reserve, by policy, maintains a more junior force than the Air Guard, and 53.5 percent who were deployed during ODS were under age 30 compared with 27.6 percent in the Air Guard. However, Marine Corps reservists are less likely to reach retirement vesting eligibility than their Air Guard counterparts. Specifically, only 2.1 percent of Marine Corps reservists had 19 YOS in the 1992 survey, while 4.5 percent of Air Guard members had 19 years. Furthermore, as shown in columns (4) and (6), of those members with 19 YOS, 20.3 percent of Air Guard members were between the ages of 51 and 60 and therefore had less than 10 years to wait before reaching age 60, the reserve retirement age. However *no member* of the Marine Reserve was in this age range. Therefore, Marine reservists with 19 years would have to wait far longer before reaching age 60.[29]

One might argue that deployed reservists will eventually become retired reservists and improved retirement benefits will reassure them that their service is valued. But again, the problem with this argument is that if one is concerned about retaining those deployed or who have a high risk of deployment, providing benefits that are deferred far into the future is a costly and poorly targeted means of doing so. As discussed earlier, other approaches such as special and incentive pay that increase current compensation are more efficient.

---

[29] Inter-service inequities also exist in the active components with respect to retirement benefits. For example, the Marine Corps maintains a more junior force than the Air Force, by policy, and Marines have a lower probability of reaching 20 years of active credible service for retirement purposes. However, deployment-related inequities in the retirement system are unique to the reserve components. We thank Paul Hogan for bringing the issue of inter-component inequality in retirement benefits to our attention.

Table 3.3

Age Distributions of Selected Reservists, Ages 18-60: Those Who Reported
Deployment During ODS; Those Reporting 19 YOS
(Percent)

Age Group	All		Marine Corps Reserve		Air Force National Guard	
	Have 19 YOS (1)	Deployed During ODS (2)	Have 19 YOS (3)	Deployed During ODS (4)	Have 19 YOS (5)	Deployed During ODS (6)
18-25	0.0	16.7	0.0	37.1	0.0	11.0
26-30	0.2	14.9	0.0	16.4	0.0	16.6
31-35	2.8	15.0	8.3	15.7	4.8	15.1
36-40	25.9	17.3	38.9	12.8	20.0	17.1
41-45	38.0	17.8	41.7	9.8	28.6	17.9
46-50	20.4	11.8	11.1	6.4	25.7	13.8
51-55	8.9	4.7	0.0	1.4	15.2	5.8
56-60	3.8	2.0	0.0	0.5	5.7	2.8

SOURCE: RCS, 1992.

Equity and Flexibility

All three of the congressional alternatives move in the direction
of greater nominal equity and flexibility. Offering reservists an
immediate annuity as is done for active-duty retirees would achieve the
greatest level of nominal equity between the reserve and active-duty
retirement systems. But this nominal equity would come at a high cost,
and nominal equity is not actual equity due to the different demands and
opportunities associated with active-duty and reserve positions. As
discussed, providing an immediate annuity to reservists, based on their
pro rata YOS, is debatably unfair to active members whose service 365
days a year involves greater total effort, risk, stress, and disruption
of family life. Furthermore, unlike their active counterparts,
reservists can qualify for civilian pension benefits, accumulating YOS
and in the case of defined contribution (DC) plans, accumulating
civilian retirement funds while serving in the military.

Moreover, retired pay is an important tool for helping the
services attract, retain, and motivate personnel and manage their career
lengths. Since active retirees typically suffer a second-career earnings
loss (relative to comparable civilian workers) when they transition to
the civilian sector (Loughran, 2001b), retired pay reduces the financial
penalty associated with the second-career phase of an active member's
career. Since reservists pursue civilian opportunities while serving,
there is a presumption that reservists do not experience a second-career
earnings loss and therefore do not need retired pay immediately upon
separation to compensate for such loss. Also, from the perspective of

force shaping, conserving trained, experienced personnel in a reserve force is prudent, as Congress observed in 1947, though it means the reserve force will tend to be older.

Recognition of the difference between actives and Reserves in the burdens placed on personnel, the force-shaping objectives, and the civilian earnings and pension accumulation opportunities leads us to a key conclusion. Whether from the viewpoints of equity or force management, there is no reason to assume that the retirement systems for the active and reserve components have to be identical.

We think the age-55 system and the sliding-age system would do little to enhance the sense of nominal equity between reserve and active retirement systems. The choices of age 55 in the age-55 system and the formula for sliding the eligibility age in the sliding-age system seem arbitrary, especially since there are no comparable age requirements found in the active retirement system. The Civil Service Retirement System (CSRS) has an eligibility age of 55 for those with 30 years of federal civil service, and one might argue for nominal equity with the civil service system in terms of age, given veterans' preference in civil service hiring and the large employment of veterans and reservists in the civil service. However, CSRS is being phased out and its replacement, the Federal Employees Retirement System (FERS), now covers the majority of civil service employees. The minimum age of retirement is rising to 57 under FERS, so age 55 will no longer be a relevant eligibility age in the civil service. Both FERS and CSRS allow those with less than 30 YOS but with at least 20 to retire at age 60, but there is no sliding-age scale based on YOS as under Bill S.1000. Thus, judged from the benchmark of FERS, none of the three congressional alternatives provides nominal equity.

The immediate annuity would enhance the overall flexibility of the compensation system. With an immediate annuity upon vesting, the components may feel freer to involuntarily separate low performers and individuals in low-demand occupations upon vesting. The immediate annuity enhances the components' ability to let personnel management objectives rather than personal compensation decisions dictate force structure.[30] It also runs the risk that some reservists will separate even though the Reserves would like them to stay. Indeed, unwanted separation of senior leaders could create problems if a large group leaves at the same time and unless the lower ranks contain a pool of well-qualified candidates to replace the personnel who separate. The age-55 and sliding-age alternatives are less successful in terms of enhancing flexibility (and run less risk of unwanted separation) since most of the involuntary separations the components might like to make are in the population age 55 and younger, and these alternatives are worth less to the reservist than the immediate annuity.

---

[30] We cannot say whether the reserve components would take advantage of this enhanced flexibility.

CHAPTER FOUR: TOWARD THE DEVELOPMENT OF RETIREMENT REFORM ALTERNATIVES

Concern about the military's retirement system is not new. Numerous study groups and commissions have discussed reforms to the system to address problems of cost, inefficiency, lack of flexibility, and inequity since the modern retirement system was created after World War II. With the exception of the sixth QRMC and some analysis for the ninth QRMC, all of these past groups focused on the active retirement system, yet many of the issues raised by these groups are relevant to the reserve components.

This concluding section discusses some of the reforms recommended by past study groups.[31] We argue that achieving a compensation system that supports the seamless integration of the active and reserve components will require reserve retirement reform to be integrated with active reform, though the resulting systems will not necessarily be identical. Furthermore, achieving meaningful reform of either system will require that the barriers to reform, such as the lack of service support for change, be addressed.

Past Proposals to Reform Reserve Retirement

Five major issues that have driven attempts at active-duty retirement reform are cost, equity, civilian comparability, force management flexibility, and selective retention. These issues all have counterparts in reserve retirement reform.

Cost

From the Hook Commission in 1948 through the adoption of REDUX in 1986, virtually all study groups were concerned about the cost of providing benefits during the second-career phase of retirement. Given that the recent congressional proposals to reduce the reserve entitlement age would effectively give benefits during some or all of reservists' second-career phase, it is ironic that all of the past studies through the 1960s, 1970s, and 1980s recommended doing the exact opposite for the active retirement system. That is, they recommended reducing, or even eliminating, the annuity for active members during this stage of their career. Some studies, like the Hook Commission in 1948 and the Joint Pay Board in 1947, recommended eliminating the annuity during the second-career phase, and therefore making the active system look more like the reserve retirement system. Others recommended reducing the annuity, and indeed one of the major changes enacted by the passage of REDUX was to cut benefits during the second-career phase by

---

[31] A complete description is provided in Christian (2003).

allowing benefits to increase by less than the CPI until age 62. The most recent study group to examine military retirement, the Defense Science Board (DSB) in 2000, rejected the notion that it was excessively costly to provide benefits during the second-career phase. They argued that if the services desired a youthful organization it was appropriate to offer a benefit that helped, and induced, members to transition to civilian life when they were in their forties and fifties. The DSB was more concerned about other issues like force management inflexibility.

Equity

Nearly all of the commissions and study groups considered the issue of equity, as have many congressional proposals introduced over the years. Of particular concern was what the Joint Pay Board called the "tontine" nature of the 20-year vesting requirement: something that benefits the surviving few at the expense of the many. Only a small fraction of personnel stay long enough in the active component or in the active and reserve components combined to qualify for benefits. A recommendation that was often put forward was to lower the vesting requirement to 10 YOS but increase the entitlement age. The Joint Pay Board recommended an entitlement age of 62 while the Retirement Modernization Act of 1974 would set it at 60. The Defense Manpower Commission in 1976 recommended that the retirement annuity be paid at age 65, with a reduced annuity at age 60. More recently, the DSB in 2000 recommended early vesting in a DC plan that would begin payout of benefits at age 62. Again, it is noteworthy that the recent congressional proposals seek to lower the reserve entitlement age while past proposals to fix the inequity of the active system recommended an increase in the entitlement age coupled with a lower vesting requirement.

Civilian Comparability

Although both the Joint Pay Board in 1947 and the President's Commission on Military Compensation in 1978 recommended providing military retirement benefits via a trust fund to which military members contribute, such contributory plans have received the greatest attention only in recent years, especially by the DSB. Driving that attention has been the dramatic growth of DC plans in the civilian sector. DC plans allow workers, once vested, to own their retirement assets. The portability of these assets supports the highly mobile workforce that characterizes the United States. It allows workers to take their benefits with them and allows employers to shed workers without being subject to the charge of opportunistic dismissal to avoid funding the retirement liabilities of the dismissed workers. It also protects workers from firm bankruptcy or under-contribution in the future, problems plaguing defined benefit plans. The Revenue Act of 1978 first allowed U.S. employers to offer 401(k) plans to their employees, and the number of U.S. employees participating in 401(k) plans rose from 4.4 million in 1983 to 23.1 million in 1993. By 1998, roughly half of all households were eligible to participate in 401(k) plans.[32] Poterba, Venti, and Wise (2000) used information on 401(k) participation and contribution patterns and found that 401(k) plans are likely to play a central role in providing for the retirement income of future retirees.

In FY2000, Congress permitted military members, including reservists, to contribute to the Thrift Savings Plan (TSP), a DC plan currently offered to federal civil service employees. However, unlike their civil service counterparts, military members receive no employer or government matching contributions. Several recent studies, including the DSB, have recommended that the military retirement system include a DC plan that is vested early and funded by DoD contributions. The DSB estimated that such a system could provide members who retire with more than 20 YOS with larger retirement benefits but cost 40 percent less than the current system. The DSB also stated that this DC system should extend to the Reserves.

Force Management Flexibility

Perhaps more than any other objective, force management flexibility has been the driving issue behind calls for retirement reform. The principal goal of military compensation is to ensure force readiness by providing a supply of members with requisite skills and experience when and where they are needed. With respect to the retirement system, early study groups focused on the importance of incentives for separation among relatively young personnel to keep the armed forces "alert and vigorous," according to the Hook Commission in 1948.

Selective Retention

The main concern regarding force management flexibility, however, was the greater than desired conformity of career lengths among military members, regardless of their occupation or specialty. The one-size-fits-all aspect of the retirement system and the strong pull of the 20-year vesting requirement for those with less than 20 YOS creates similarity in the experience mix of personnel across occupational areas and hampers the ability of the services to manage areas differently. Later commissions and study groups understood the value of giving the services the flexibility to manage skills separately. The Retirement Modernization Act of 1974 proposed a system of voluntary and involuntary separation payments. The Defense Manpower Commission in 1976 proposed a

---

[32] Information and discussion of the growth of 401(k) plans are found in

point system for the receipt of annuity benefits for active members, with those in combat roles having the ability to earn points at a faster rate than those in noncombat roles. During the defense drawdown in the early 1990s, following the end of the Cold War, the voluntary separation incentive and special separation benefit were used by the services to target the separation of personnel in specific occupations in a specific year of service and pay-grade groups. These incentives were tremendously successful in achieving dramatic reductions in end-strength, especially in the Army and Air Force, while providing members with a benefit that eased their transition to civilian life. They were also highly effective at targeting the separation of lower quality personnel in terms of Armed Forces Qualification Test (AFQT) score and high school diploma status (Asch and Warner, 2001).

To address the lack of flexibility embedded in the retirement system, the DSB in 2000 recommended a permanent system of separation benefits. The benefits would be an annuity based on the current retirement system formula (high-three) and would be received from separation to age 62. At 62, the individual could draw from his or her TSP fund. The separation benefits could be used to achieve differing career lengths in different skill areas. Areas where a shorter career is sufficient, such as combat arms, would receive the benefit early on when they are younger. Areas where longer careers are desirable, such as computer programmers, could begin receipt at older ages. In this way the retirement system would achieve its two-fold purpose: helping members to accumulate savings for retirement (via the thrift saving plan vested early and paying benefits at age 62) and helping the services flexibly manage their personnel (via a system of separation annuities paid from the date of separation until age 62).

Relevance of Proposals to Reserve Retirement Reform

The issues surrounding the active retirement system are relevant to if not always on the forefront of concerns driving reserve retirement reform. In many ways the issues that concerned past study groups and commissions regarding the active retirement system differ substantially from those driving the concern about the reserve system, discussed in Section 2. While equity is of concern for the reserve system, the issue is equity vis-à-vis the active system and the integration of the two systems, not equity vis-à-vis those who do and do not reach the 20-year vesting point. Nonetheless, the 20-year vesting rule is a component of the reserve system and therefore, arguably, is an equity issue in the Reserves as well as in the active components. Similarly, management flexibility is of concern in the reserve components, but the issue in ·

Poterba, Venti, and Wise (1998, 2000) and Papke (1995, 1999).

the Reserves revolves around assuring the retention of trained personnel but preventing "superannuation" caused by weak incentives to leave the Reserves after reaching 20 YOS. In the active components, the issue revolves around the uniformity of career lengths and the one-size-fits-all career produced by the active retirement system. Nonetheless, uniformity of career lengths across skill areas within components is relevant to the Reserves as well. Comparability with the private sector and the call for 401(k) plans with matching contributions is another issue that has sparked debate about the active system, yet has been muted in debates about the reserve system.[33] Again, this issue is relevant to the Reserves as well because the reserve system, like the active system, is a defined benefit, not a DC plan, and currently member contributions to TSP funds are not matched by DoD.

Conclusions

Our review of past proposals and initiatives leads to two other conclusions for reserve retirement reform.

First, to support the total-force concept, it is clear that retirement reform for both the active and reserve components must work in concert to achieve their respective personnel goals. The idea of total-force management, along with the seamless integration of the active and reserve components, has received considerable attention in the past decade, and especially since September 11, 2001. Although the retirement systems for the components need not be identical, alternatives to reform either system should be judged in terms of how they support the total force. Therefore, proposals such as the one by the DSB that call for a 401(k)-type plan (e.g., a TSP and system of separation pay) should be assessed not only in terms of their effect on active personnel outcomes, such as retention and cost, but also on reserve outcomes, such as reserve affiliation, retention, and cost. Similarly, proposals such as the four recent congressional bills that seek to reduce the age of entitlement of reserve retirement benefits should consider their effects on active members, especially in terms of equity. The goal of our larger project is to use the DRM to provide a total force assessment of alternative proposals. The assessment will include estimates of changes in active and reserve retention, personnel cost, and reserve affiliation.

---

[33] An exception is the debate in 1999 about whether reservists should be allowed to participate in the TSP that was to be provided in FY2000 for active members. The concern of the TSP investment board was that participation and levels of contributions of reservists would be low, yet the cost of administering their fund accumulations would be high. Ultimately, it was decided to include reservists in the legislation that

Second, in addition to considering the total force implications, assessments of alternative proposals should also consider how to address the obstacles to reform. Despite the numerous recommendations to structurally change the military retirement system made over the years by the many studies and commissions, the system, in fact, has changed very little. Changes that were made in 1981, 1986, and 2000 (see Appendix A) did not respond to the primary concerns expressed by the study groups about equity, flexibility, and the cost of the system in the second-career phase. Mostly, the changes to high-three in 1981 and to the REDUX annuity formula in 1986 were viewed as cost-cutting moves. In fact, the changes in the system in 2000 restored the high-three option for those covered by REDUX. Clearly, there are obstacles to reform.

What are these obstacles? A full accounting is beyond the scope of this paper, but one obstacle is the lack of consensus for change. As discussed in Asch and Hosek (2004), the call for retirement reform has not been voiced by the services, and the gains in military capability from reform have not been quantified. Furthermore, a transition plan has not been specified and the costs of the transition have not been estimated. To some, any revamping of the retirement system raises fears of broken trust, benefit cuts, and an open door to future rounds of disruptive and demoralizing changes. To overcome the inherent obstacles to change, proposals to reform the retirement system should not only efficiently meet the compensation and personnel goals of the active and reserve components, they should also be politically feasible, analytically rigorous, and compelling, if actual reform is to occur.

---

permitted military members to contribute to the TSP (see Asch and Warner, 2000).

APPENDIX A: THE RESERVE AND ACTIVE-DUTY RETIREMENT SYSTEMS

Members of the reserve components who accumulate 20 YCS with the last eight years of qualifying service in the Ready Reserve[34] are entitled to receive retired pay beginning at age 60.[35] No retirement pay is provided to members separating from the Reserves with less than 20 calendar YOS. Retired pay at age 60 is calculated based on YCS when transferred from the Ready Reserve and basic pay as calculated under one of several methods discussed below:

$$Y = YCS \times 0.025 \times BP \qquad (1)$$

where Y is monthly retired pay and BP is monthly basic pay. Roughly speaking, YCS is a prorated number of calendar YOS. Specifically, YCS is calculated by dividing a reservist's accumulated retirement points by 360. Retirement points are computed as follows:

- One point for each day of active-duty service
- One point for each period of inactive-duty training (IDT)
- One point for each day in funeral honors duty status
- One point for each accredited three-credit-hour correspondence course satisfactorily completed
- Fifteen points for each year of active status membership in a reserve component

Under current law, reservists may accumulate no more than 90 inactive-duty points (annual membership, IDT, and course-credit points) and a total 365 active- and inactive-duty points combined in a single year. The restriction on inactive-duty points has been relaxed significantly in recent years. Prior to retirement years ending September 23, 1996, annual inactive-duty points were capped at 60. This limit increased to 75 points for retirement years ending between September 23, 1996, and October 30, 2000, and stands at 90 points for years after October 30, 2000. There is also a career limit on retirement points of 10,950, or 30 YCS. A minimum of 50 points must be earned in a year for that year to count toward meeting the 20 calendar YOS minimum for vesting in retired pay. The average enlisted reservist separating

---

[34] The Ready Reserves encompasses the Selected Reserve, the Individual Ready Reserve, and the Inactive National Guard. It excludes the Retired Reserves.

from the Ready Reserve in FY2000 had accumulated 2,984 retirement points over 25 calendar years of active-duty and reserve service. The average reserve officer retiring in FY2000 had accumulated 3,585 retirement points over 27 calendar YOS. Median retirement point accumulation among all reservists totaled 77 for enlisted members and 79 for officers in FY2000.

The computation of *BP* depends on when the reserve member first entered military service and whether he or she transferred to the Retired Reserve upon separating from the Ready Reserve. For members entering prior to September 8, 1980, *BP* is the basic pay in effect for a given rank and calendar YOS when the member first begins to receive retired pay. Importantly, a member can continue to accumulate calendar YOS (i.e., longevity) for the purposes of computing *BP* if he or she transfers to the Retired Reserve after separating from the Ready Reserve. Consequently, individuals who separate from the Ready Reserve prior to reaching the highest level of basic pay for a given rank can increase *BP* by remaining in the Retired Reserve. Members of the Retired Reserve are not required to participate in drilling or training but can be called to active duty without consent in the interest of national defense. They receive no compensation and do not accumulate retirement points.

For members who enter on or after September 8, 1980, *BP* is computed as the average of the highest 36 months of basic pay ("high-three averaging"). For reservists who transfer to the Retired Reserve, high-three averaging takes place over basic pay in their last three YOS in the Retired Reserve (typically ages 57-59). For reservists who end their affiliation with the Reserves upon separation from the Ready Reserve, *BP* is calculated over their last three YOS in the Ready Reserve. This distinction creates very strong incentives for reservists to remain in the Retired Reserve until age 60 so that *BP* at age 60 reflects real-wage growth subsequent to separation from the Ready Reserve as well as any increases in pay due to changes in longevity. There is no incentive to delay retirement beyond age 60. All members below major general must separate by age 60 and limits on calendar YOS may force some reservists to separate before age 60. Retired pay beginning at age 60 for all members is adjusted for inflation according to changes in the CPI for urban wage earners.

In Chapter 2 of the main text we make comparisons between reserve and active-duty retirement systems, so it is worth highlighting the primary differences between the two retirement systems. The most significant difference between the two retirement systems is that

---

[35] Between October 1994 and September 2001, the number of qualifying

active-duty members with 20 or more calendar YOS begin receiving retirement pay immediately upon separating from the active-duty force instead of at age 60 as under the reserve retirement system. There are also differences in the formula used to convert YCS and basic pay to retirement pay, the most important being that YCS equals years of calendar service for active-duty members.

There are currently three different systems under which active-duty retirement pay can be calculated. For members entering military service prior to September 8, 1980, active-duty retirement pay is computed using the formula in Equation (1), and *BP* is simply basic pay on the date of separation.[36] For members entering military service between September 8, 1980, and July 31, 1986, *BP* is calculated under the high-three averaging method discussed above. Under both of these systems, annual retirement pay is adjusted according to changes in the CPI urban wage-earners series.

Active-duty members who enter military service after July 31, 1986, must choose between two retirement systems in their fifteenth year of service. The first system is identical to the high-three averaging system. The second system is known as REDUX. Under REDUX, active-duty members receive a $30,000 career-retention bonus at 15 YOS. Their initial retirement pay is then calculated according to the following formula:

$$Y = [0.40 + 0.035(YCS - 20)] \times BP \tag{2}$$

where *BP* is calculated under high-three averaging. Between the year of retirement and age 62, retirement pay under REDUX is adjusted according to the CPI minus 1 percent. At age 62, REDUX makes two adjustments to retirement pay. The first is to adjust the multiplier to what it would have been had the member retired under the high-three averaging system. For example, a member retiring under REDUX with 20 YOS would receive 40 percent of *BP* between retirement and age 62 and 50 percent of *BP* thereafter. The second adjustment is to restore retirement pay to what it would have been had retirement pay been fully indexed to the CPI. Thus, at age 62, retirement pay is identical under REDUX and the high-three averaging system. After age 62, however, retirement pay under REDUX is once again adjusted according to the CPI minus 1 percent. There are no data available on what percentage of active-duty members choose REDUX over high-three averaging since the first eligible cohort is just attaining 15 YOS. In its annual projections of pension costs, DoD's

---

years was reduced from eight to six.

[36] Calendar years of service are capped at 30 under all three systems.

Office of the Actuary assumes that 48 percent of enlisted members and 42 percent of officers will choose to retire under REDUX.

APPENDIX B: PRINCIPLES OF MILITARY COMPENSATION

The following is a list of general compensation principles as outlined in the fifth edition of the *Military Compensation Background Papers* (U.S. DoD, 1996) and specific reserve retirement reform principles as outlined by the sixth QRMC (U.S. DoD, 1988).

General Principles of Military Compensation (fifth edition of the *Military Compensation Background Papers*, Chapter One [U.S. DoD, 1996]).

1. ***MANPOWER/COMPENSATION INTERRELATIONSHIP.*** The first principle underlying the basic philosophy of the military compensation system is that the system must be an integral part of the overall system by which military manpower is managed. Compensation, by the very nature of its basic purpose, must support defense manpower policies, which, in turn, support the military, strategic and operational plans of this nation. If they do not, then manpower imbalances, deteriorating unit cohesion and integrity, poor morale, and a general degradation of discipline and motivation are likely to ensue. This in turn can frustrate the successful accomplishment of strategic and operational plans in the field, and thus negate our foreign policy objectives. Compensation for members of the armed forces, therefore, must be synchronized with the rest of the military manpower system and not be treated as an isolated part of the national labor market. This basic principle of compensation was implied in the Presidential memorandum establishing the Fifth QRMC in which it was understood that military compensation is and should remain an integral part of military activities. The importance of this principle can be appreciated when reviewing the suggestions of various critics of military compensation. These critics view military compensation as an autonomous system, unrelated to other military operations, and thus a logical candidate for the supply-and-demand labor market analysis often applied to the private sector by the same critics.

2. ***COMPATIBILITY WITH TECHNOLOGY AND TACTICS.*** Military compensation should reflect the realities of the high level technology employed by the armed forces and the combat tactics of today's battlefield environment. This refers to the inevitable time-lag between the realities of the battlefield and the systems, such as compensation, designed to support the combat forces. The effect of changing combat tactics (often resulting from the characteristics of new weapons) is most noticeable in certain special and incentive pays (e.g., aviation pays) but permeate the military compensation systems. The introduction of newer, high-performance weapons and their effects on combat tactics was the reason why long-term reviews of military compensation were instituted in the first place. The importance of keeping military compensation in synchronization with changing combat tactics is a cardinal precept that cannot be overstressed.

3. ***EQUITY.*** The third principle is that of equity, in the sense of "fairness." Few things are more important for morale than that service members believe that they are being treated as fairly as possible and, conversely, few things undermine morale more than a sense of unfair treatment. This principle requires that all service members be allowed to compete equally for pay and promotion according to their own abilities. This principle applies equally to the Regular, Reserve, and retired forces whose combined strength constitutes the backbone of our national security. This principle also deals with the concept of equal pay for substantially equal work under the same general working

conditions. This aspect of the equity principle establishes the basis for the two important sub-principles of pay: comparability and competitiveness.

a. *Comparability.* The basis for determining the appropriate pay levels for the service-specific aspects of the compensation of the uniformed services should be comparability with the American economy. This addresses the question: "How much should service members be paid?" by answering, "About the same as their approximate counterparts (in terms of function and responsibility) are paid in the American economy." The specific items referred to here are basic pay, basic-pay-related items, the allowances, and benefits. This also responds to the main reason articulated in international law pertaining to why service members wear distinguishing uniforms, which is to differentiate between armed combatants and noncombatants. This distinction implies that the major difference is that members of the armed forces are legally liable to armed combat. This is their distinguishing characteristic, and whatever specialization for specific duties a member of an armed force may have is secondary to the primary function of armed combat. Hence, the fact that basic pay rates are the same for each grade and longevity step recognizes this basic function.

Much of the controversy over the comparability principle has arisen because of the different meanings attached to the word and to the perception that comparability means "sameness" or "exactness." Many consider that comparability implies that military duties are exactly the same as civilian jobs and that civilians use and intend the word to mean equal or identical pay. Including the word "substantially" in the definition "equal pay for substantially equal work" recognizes that there are different conditions of employment between any two organizations, and that it would be fruitless to attempt to locate exactly equal work for comparison with Federal civilian workers. The British recognize that an exact comparison between military and civilian jobs is unnecessary as a condition for using that comparison in setting pay levels for their service members. Quoting from a report on their pay system:

There is obviously no basis for comparing civilian jobs with jobs like infantryman and gunner, for which there are no civilian counterparts; or even with pilots, seamen, policemen, nurses, cooks and others with similarly denominated civilian jobs, but which are frequently very different jobs in civilian life. However, all jobs, whether service or civilian, possess certain common demands for which any employer is willing to pay wages. These demands can be assessed and given values as proportions of a whole job. The important ones like knowledge, mental or physical skills and demand, or responsibility, are obvious, and there are many others, some of which are of little consequence in differentiating between the sizes of jobs. What is intended is that members of the armed forces should be paid generally what they might fairly expect were they to apply the knowledge, skill, and responsibility of their Service jobs to jobs required to be done in the civilian life.

b. *Competitiveness.* Compensation competitiveness is needed to ensure the adequate manning of certain military specialties. This subprinciple applies to special and incentive pays, particularly in peacetime. "Competitiveness" refers to both external (i.e., private market pressures) and internal competition (i.e., those military duties requiring volunteer manning because of their hazardous, arduous, uncomfortable, long training lead-time, and/or high training investment characteristics). Competitiveness includes those bonuses and special pays that can and will be discontinued during major mobilization and wartime. This is possible because the competitiveness for attraction would likely be negated by a draft, and competitiveness for retention is nullified through "stop-loss" and retirement denial policies. During peacetime, such special and incentive pays are needed for specific duties that are in high demand in the economy, that are inherently more dangerous than most peacetime duties, or that are just uncomfortable and unattractive.

4. ***EFFECTIVENESS IN PEACE AND WAR.*** The fourth guiding principle for the military compensation system is that *it must operate effectively in both peace and war.* This principle suggests that one military compensation system is required because there will be no time to switch systems in wartime (even if that course were theoretically desirable). Further, any system must be flexible enough to permit the entry and departure in both peace and war situations of reservists and retirees in a way that will not confuse their promotion patterns, retirement credit, and various related compensation elements. This has significant implications for any proposal to adopt a salary system, for example. Any military compensation system must be designed to allow for rapid and smooth expansions and contractions of the force. Military personnel should be allowed to concentrate on their duties without having to adapt to changes in a system that is supposed to support them, not hinder them.

In line with this latter principle, the military compensation system should accommodate mobilization planning, promotion patterns, force levels and training lead-times of the Department of Defense. Many proposals for the "reform" of the compensation system ignore mobilization plans; and, indeed, the existing structure does so to some degree by requiring congressional action to terminate or install certain items in the event of mobilization or war. Such times are the least propitious moments to effect the needed changes in a thoughtful manner. It would be far preferable to enact provisions that allow the necessary steps to be taken administratively.

5. ***FLEXIBILITY.*** The fifth principle underlying the overall compensation system is that it ought to be designed in a way to adjust quickly to changing conditions of combat tactics, technology, and manpower supply and demand. Here again, there are several subprinciples involved. An effective system cannot be designed without a reasonable specification of the force size and manpower profile that the system is to support; *i.e.,* a definitive statement of manpower requirements is needed which has as its foundation reasonable standards.

a. ***Efficiency.*** The subprinciple of efficiency deals with the concept of economic efficiency. The amount or level of military compensation should be no higher or lower than necessary to fulfill the basic objective of attracting, retaining, and motivating the kinds and numbers of Service personnel needed for the active and Reserve forces of the United States.

b. ***Supply and Demand.*** Differing manpower supply conditions (skill and experience profiles) and demand conditions (desired force profiles) among the uniformed services, for both the regular and the Reserve forces, require a system with flexibility and a broad pricing base to satisfy the varying needs of different military situations. Special and incentive pays, which are the basic compensation tools employed to satisfy this principle are, if nonfunctional, inconsistent with efficient compensation practices.

c. ***Linkage of Elements ("Drag-Alongs").*** When a rigid linkage of compensation elements exists (as whenever one element, such as basic pay, changes, it automatically causes a similar change in a half-dozen or more other compensation elements), it generally creates inefficiencies because of differing needs served by each element. Such linkages (often called "drag-alongs") should not be a part of the basic compensation system design, unless the respective elements are clearly driven by the same criterion.

d. ***Rapid and Equitable Adjustments.*** The compensation system should have a rapid and equitable adjustment mechanism to reflect changes in the national economy. Service members must receive sufficient compensation to enable them to establish standards of living that will allow the simultaneous discharge of their responsibilities to their country and to their families. The compensation system of the uniformed services should, therefore, be related to the state of the national economy so that its members may participate in the gradual rise in the standard of living.

6. ***MOTIVATIONAL ASPECTS.*** The sixth, and last, principle relates to the need to incorporate into the system a relationship between compensation and the effort, or contribution, required of the individual. The basic system, as well as any special or supplemental aspects, should be designed to encourage meritorious performance and advancement to higher responsibilities. There are several associated subprinciples:

a. ***Institutional Benefits.*** The overall institutional benefits component of the military compensation system should be awarded according to the military value of the member to the Service. This subprinciple provides a guide to the recipients in regard to approximate levels of benefits. Many benefits, however, are (and should be) automatic in their entitlement, such as Dependency and Indemnity Compensation, Death Gratuity, and the group insurance programs. Nonetheless, the criterion of military value, including the possibility of mobilization or recall to active duty in times of national emergency, should govern the eligibility for and level of benefits to the various categories of beneficiaries.

b. ***Distinctiveness.*** The overall compensation system must reflect the distinctive characteristics of serving in the armed forces. The very essence of this distinctiveness is that members of the armed forces must be able to engage in mortal combat and put their lives in jeopardy. The services can scarcely be manned with members possessing the alertness and vitality needed to be able to provide the leadership necessary to win wars unless service members are compelled to leave active service at reasonable ages or sooner if no longer sufficiently competitive. This requires a system of severance and retirement compensation that is designed to meet the many problems of superannuation. The theory underlying the solution to this problem, which is not only one of age but of other factors affecting ability and competence, must make sense to the intelligent citizen who finally pays the cost. This aspect of the compensation system should be viewed by most rational people as being "good business" despite the associated cost. The compensation subprinciples that underlie the military retirement system are as follows: (1) the system should be structured to meet legitimate defense requirements, such as recall to active duty of some or all retired members, in support of our national security objectives; (2) the system should support and complement force management requirements (e.g., youth, vigor, and career development opportunities) of the active and Reserve components of the armed forces; and (3) the system should be integrated into the military compensation system and be structured to meet an income replacement function as well as an income maintenance function acceptable to the Nation.

Principals of Reserve Retirement Reform (sixth QRMC, V1B, Chapter Six [U.S. DoD, 1988]).

1. The reserve retirement system must be fully compatible with the active-duty retirement system, with active-duty and reserve service creditable in either system.

2. Reserve retirement should be sufficiently attractive to aid in recruiting members with prior active component service without being so competitive that it causes undesired attrition from the active component.

3. An alternative system should be structured to support the accomplishment of reserve manpower force objective in the near term.

4. Members who first entered a uniformed service prior to the enactment of any proposed alternative should be provided the option of electing the alternative system or remaining under the current system.

5. An alternative system must be sufficiently flexible to meet the needs of all seven reserve components.

6. The economic incentive for any desirable alternative should always be for continued service in a pay billet through, at minimum, 30 years of service.

7. An alternative to the current retirement system should provide an incentive for continuous satisfactory service from initial entry through, at minimum, 2 years of service.

8. An alternative to the retirement system should provide a means to replace an appropriate percentage of reserve compensation for members who have qualified for retirement at age 60 but can no longer participate due to policy or personal reasons.

9. An alternative should be relatively straightforward in application, so that the modified or optional system can be readily communicated to and understood by reserve members.

Retirement system alternatives should be cost neutral or reduce long-term retired pay costs.

APPENDIX C: DATA

This report relies primarily on data on selected reservists from the RCCPDS. The RCCPDS assembles administrative data on the reserve population reported by each reserve component on a monthly basis. We use the September 1987, 1991, 1995, and 1999 master RCCPDS data files in this report. The September 1999 RCCPDS data file contains records on 894,320 selected reservists. Table A-1 tabulates some characteristics of reservists with 20 or more YOS.

In addition, we use the annual transaction file from FY2000 to determine which reservists serving in the Selected Reserve in September 1999 separated from the Selected Reserve in FY2000. We assume any individual with 20 or more YOS (the last eight or more of which were in the Selected Reserve) with a transaction code indicating transfer to civilian life, transfer to the Retired Reserve, transfer to inactive duty, or involuntary retirement separated in FY2000 eligible to receive retirement pay at age 60. Table C-2 tabulates some characteristics of these reservists.

Table C.1

Reserve Characteristics by YOS

YOS	Modal Rank	2004 Basic Pay Current ($)	2004 Basic Pay Maximum Longevity ($)	Median Age	Life Expectancy
20	O-5	6390	6761	45	78
21	O-5	6563	6761	46	78
22	O-5	6563	6761	47	78
23	O-5	6761	6761	48	78
24	O-5	6761	6761	49	79
25	O-5	6761	6761	49	79
26	O-5	6761	6761	50	79
27	O-5	6761	6761	50	79
28	O-5	6761	6761	50	79
29	O-6	8285	8285	52	79
30	O-6	8285	8285	53	79
31	O-6	8285	8285	54	79
32	O-6	8285	8285	54	79
33	O-6	8285	8285	55	79
34	O-6	8285	8285	56	80
20	E-6	2810	2810	44	78
21	E-6	2810	2810	45	78
22	E-6	2810	2810	46	78
23	E-7	3498	3855	48	78
24	E-7	3498	3855	48	78
25	E-7	3599	3855	50	79
26	E-7	3599	3855	50	79
27	E-7	3855	3855	50	79
28	E-7	3855	3855	51	79
29	E-7	3855	3855	51	79
30	E-7	3855	3855	52	79
31	E-7	3855	3855	53	79
32	E-7	3855	3855	53	79
33	E-7	3855	3855	54	79
34	E-8	4314	4314	57	80

SOURCE: FY1999 RCCPDS. Notes: Sample includes individuals serving last eight years or more in the Selected Reserve.

Table C.2

Characteristics of Reserve Retirees

| AGE | YOS | Modal Rank | 2004 Basic Pay | | Median Point Accumulation | Life Expectancy | Number of Retirees |
			Current	Maximum Longevity			
37	20	O-4	$5,733	$5,733	1,896	77	3
38	20	O-4	$5,733	$5,733	2,756	77	15
39	20	O-4	$5,733	$5,733	2,493	78	20
40	20	O-4	$5,733	$5,733	3,016	78	39
41	21	O-4	$5,733	$5,733	2,958	78	49
42	21	O-4	$5,733	$5,733	3,234	78	87
43	21	O-5	$6,563	$6,761	3,579	78	145
44	21	O-5	$6,563	$6,761	3,868	78	150
45	21	O-5	$6,563	$6,761	4,135	78	162
46	22	O-5	$6,563	$6,761	3,601	78	154
47	22	O-5	$6,563	$6,761	3,445	78	165
48	24	O-5	$6,761	$6,761	3,346	78	169
49	24	O-5	$6,761	$6,761	3,255	79	277
50	25	O-5	$6,761	$6,761	3,146	79	313
51	26	O-5	$6,761	$6,761	3,072	79	294
52	27	O-6	$8,285	$8,285	3,310	79	313
53	27	O-6	$8,285	$8,285	3,257	79	189
54	28	O-6	$8,285	$8,285	3,395	79	136
55	29	O-6	$8,285	$8,285	3,271	79	102
56	29	O-6	$8,285	$8,285	3,384	80	69
57	28	O-6	$8,285	$8,285	3,193	80	55
58	27	O-6	$8,285	$8,285	3,388	80	46
59	27	O-6	$8,285	$8,285	3,398	80	111
60	28	O-6	$8,285	$8,285	3,311	80	16
37	20	E-7	$3,296	$3,855	1,705	77	50
38	20	E-6	$2,810	$2,810	1,724	77	247
39	20	E-6	$2,810	$2,810	1,982	78	377
40	20	E-6	$2,810	$2,810	2,457	78	460
41	20	E-6	$2,810	$2,810	2,660	78	433
42	21	E-6	$2,810	$2,810	2,563	78	461
43	21	E-6	$2,421	$2,421	2,648	78	472
44	21	E-6	$2,810	$2,810	2,723	78	404
45	21	E-6	$2,810	$2,810	2,563	78	372
46	22	E-6	$2,810	$2,810	2,736	78	373
47	22	E-6	$2,810	$2,810	2,597	78	386
48	22	E-7	$3,342	$3,855	2,486	78	381
49	22	E-6	$2,810	$2,810	2,609	79	407
50	22	E-7	$3,342	$3,855	2,574	79	466
51	23	E-7	$3,498	$3,855	2,615	79	452
52	23	E-7	$3,498	$3,855	2,734	79	519
53	23	E-6	$2,810	$2,810	2,819	79	353
54	22	E-7	$3,342	$3,855	2,719	79	300
55	24	E-7	$3,498	$3,855	2,871	79	272
56	23	E-6	$2,810	$2,810	2,813	80	258
57	24	E-7	$3,498	$3,855	2,883	80	198
58	24	E-7	$3,498	$3,855	3,003	80	163
59	25	E-7	$3,599	$3,855	3,006	80	713
60	25	E-7	$3,599	$3,855	2,845	80	119

SOURCE: FY1999 and FY2000 RCCPDS. Notes: Sample includes individuals with at least 20 YOS and last eight years or more in the Selected Reserve who separated from the Selected Reserve in FY2000.

REFERENCES

Asch, Beth, and James Hosek, *Looking to the Future: What Does Transformation Mean for Military Manpower and Personnel Policy?* Santa Monica, Calif.: RAND Corporation, OP-108-OSD, 2004.

Asch, Beth, James Hosek, Daniel Clendenning, and Michael Mattock, *Extending the Dynamic Retention Model to Include the Reserve Components,* Santa Monica, Calif.: RAND Corporation, PM-1623-OSD, 2003.

Asch, Beth, Richard Johnson, and John Warner, *Reforming the Military Retirement System,* Santa Monica, Calif.: RAND Corporation, MR-809-OSD, 1998.

Asch, Beth, and John Warner, *A Policy Analysis of Alternative Military Retirement Systems,* Santa Monica, Calif.: RAND Corporation, MR-465-OSD, 1994.

Asch, Beth, and John Warner, *The Thrift Savings Plan: Will Reservists Participate?* Santa Monica, Calif.: RAND Corporation, DB-306-OSD, 2000.

Asch, Beth, and John Warner, *An Examination of the Effects of Voluntary Separation Incentives,* Santa Monica, Calif.: RAND Corporation, MR-859-OSD, 2001.

Christian, John, *An Overview of Past Proposals for Military Retirement Reform,* Santa Monica, Calif.: RAND Corporation, PM-1616-OSD, 2003.

ESGR (Employer Support for the Guard and Reserve), "The Law/USERRA," http://www.esgr.org/employers2/thelaw.asp (as of February 2, 2004).

Fricker, Ronald, *The Effects of Perstempo on Officer Retention in the U.S. Military,* Santa Monica, Calif.: RAND Corporation, MR-1556-OSD, 2002.

Hosek, James, Beth Asch, C. Christine Fair, Craig Martin, and Michael Mattock, *Married to the Military: The Employment and Earnings of Military Wives Compared with Those of Civilian Wives,* Santa Monica, Calif.: RAND Corporation, MR-1565-OSD, 2002.

Hosek, James, and Mark Totten, *Does Perstempo Hurt Reenlistment? The Effect of Long or Hostile Perstempo on Reenlistment,* Santa Monica, Calif.: RAND Corporation, MR-990-OSD, 1998.

Hosek, James, and Mark Totten, *Serving Away from Home: How Deployments Influence Reenlistment,* Santa Monica, Calif.: RAND Corporation, MR-1594-OSD, 2002.

Loeb, Vernon, "Army Reserve Chief Fears Retention Crisis," *Washington Post,* January 21, 2004, p. 4.

Loughran, David, *Reforming the Reserve Retirement System,* Santa Monica, Calif.: RAND Corporation, PM-1278-OSD, 2001a.

Loughran, David, *Wage Growth in the Civilian Careers of Military Retirees,* Santa Monica, Calif.: RAND Corporation, MR-1363-OSD, 2001b.

Loughran, David, Jacob Alex Klerman, and Craig Martin *Activation and the Earnings of Reservists*, Santa Monica, Calif.: RAND Corporation, MG-474-OSD, 2006.

Milgrom, Paul, "Employment Contracts, Influence Activities, and Efficient Organization Design," *Journal of Political Economy,* Vol. 96, No. 1, 1988, pp. 42–60.

Office of the Assistant Secretary of Defense for Reserve Affairs, *Review of Reserve Component Contributions to National Defense,* Washington, D.C., December 20, 2002.

Office of the Under Secretary of Defense for Acquisition, Technology, and Logistics, *Report of the Defense Science Board Task Force on Human Resources Strategy,* Washington, D.C., February 2000.

Papke, Leslie E., "Are 401(k) Plans Replacing Other Employer-Provided Pensions: Evidence from Panel Data," *Journal of Human Resources,* Vol. 34, No. 2, 1995, pp. 311–325.

Papke, Leslie E., "Participation in and Contributions to 401(k) Pension Plans: Evidence from Plan Data," *Journal of Human Resources,* Vol. 30, No. 2, 1999, pp. 346–368.

Poterba, James, Steven Venti, and David Wise, "401(k) Plans and Future Patterns of Retirement Savings," *American Economic Review,* Vol. 88, No. 2, Papers and Proceedings of the Hundred and Tenth Annual Meetings of the American Economic Association, May 1998, pp. 179–184.

Poterba, James, Steven Venti, and David Wise, "Saver Behavior and 401(k) Retirement Wealth," *American Economic Review,* Vol. 90, No. 2, Papers and Proceedings of the Hundred Twelfth Annual Meetings of the American Economic Association, May 2000, pp. 297–302.

United States Department of Defense, *Sixth Quadrennial Review of Military Compensation,* Vol. 1B, Washington, D.C., U.S. Government Printing Office, 1988.

United States Department of Defense, *Military Compensation Background Papers,* 5th Edition, Washington, D.C., U.S. Government Printing Office, 1996.

U.S. General Accounting Office, *Military Personnel: DOD Needs More Data to Address Financial and Health Care Issues Affecting Reservists,* GAO-03-1004, Washington, D.C., September 2003.

Warner, John T., and Saul Pleeter, "The Personal Discount Rate: Evidence from Military Downsizing Programs," *American Economic Review,* Vol. 91, No. 1, 2001, pp. 33–53.